152

WILD

things to do

THE wildlife TRUSTS

E&T

First published 2010 by Elliott and Thompson Limited
27 John Street, London WC1N 2BX
www.eandtbooks.com

ISBN: 9781904027898

Cover images: iStockphoto/Matthew Dixon, Andrew Pearson,
Emma Bradshaw and Shutterstock/mycteria

9 8 7 6 5 4 3 2 1

A CIP catalogue record for this book is
available from the British Library

Printed in Italy by Printer Trento on sustainable paper

FSC
Mixed Sources
Product group from well-managed
forests and other controlled sources
Cert no. CQ-COC-000012
www.fsc.org
© 1996 Forest Stewardship Council

THE WILDLIFE TRUSTS

By the 1960s, in response to the widespread devastation of our natural habitats, Wildlife Trusts had been formed across the length and breadth of the UK. Ancient woodlands, wildflower meadows, lakes, mosses, moors, islands, estuaries and beaches were all rescued in an urgent drive to save our natural heritage for future generations.

Today there are 47 individual Wildlife Trusts covering the whole of the UK and collectively we have nearly 800,000 members. We manage more than 2,250 nature reserves and every year we advise thousands of landowners on how to manage their land for wildlife. We run marine conservation projects around the UK, collecting vital data on the state of our seas and celebrating our amazing marine wildlife. Every year we work with thousands of schools and our nature reserves and visitor centres receive millions of visitors.

Our many nature reserves are the cornerstone for our vision of A Living Landscape. This is The Wildlife Trusts' recovery plan for the UK's wildlife and fragmented natural habitats. We are working with landowners across the UK to create large areas in which wildlife flourishes, helping to safeguard the ecosystems we depend on for natural services like clean air, carbon storage and water.

We are at the forefront of marine conservation in the UK, campaigning for Living Seas, surveying marine wildlife and protecting nature reserves around the coast, home to wildlife such as seabirds and seals as well as being great places for a spot of rockpooling and family days out.

So if you're after somewhere to take the family or want to go in search of rare plants and animals, if you fancy brushing up on your birdwatching skills or trying some wildlife photography, your local Wildlife Trust will be caring for places near you, for you.

We couldn't do our work without the support of our members. If you'd like to join your local Wildlife Trust and help us to protect wildlife and wild places, visit www.wildlifetrusts.org/yourlocaltrust or call 01636 677711. Or contact your local Trust directly.

VEOLIA
ENVIRONNEMENT

We are extremely proud to sponsor this wonderful book which encourages people to take small steps to protect, enhance and enjoy the natural world around them. Our staff have also contributed to the content of this book through competitions run within our Group – see pages 176 and 226.

Our involvement in this book complements our commitment to both the environment and biodiversity and demonstrates our willingness to support sustainable development. It also embodies our corporate values including the preservation of natural resources and the very real need to educate and inspire people of all ages.

Across our Group we support a wide range of environmentally focused projects, initiatives and charities including being the title sponsor of the Natural History Museum's prestigious Wildlife Photographer of the Year competition.

Over the years we have worked with The Wildlife Trusts on numerous worthwhile and valuable projects that have helped make a difference. We hope that this book will inspire people up and down the country to enjoy and protect the natural beauty and richness of nature which can often be found on our doorstep.

Kevin Hurst
Marketing and Communications Director
www.veolia.co.uk

CONTENTS

SPRING p1

SUMMER p58

AUTUMN p112

WINTER p168

HOW TO USE THIS GUIDE

152 Wild Things to Do is a practical guide designed to help you get closer to nature, wherever you are in the UK. We couldn't fit everything in, but we hope that there is plenty here to get you started. The 47 Wildlife Trusts around the UK have each contributed an idea for something wild to do in their area, so wherever you live, there should be something for you.

The book is not in any particular order, so simply dip in and out as you like to find ideas that suit you. It is very loosely grouped by season, but while some things can only be done at certain times, others can be enjoyed at any time of year. The map overleaf shows you where each of the Wildlife Trust site-specific entries are.

Some of the things to do in the book may not be suitable for all ages and may require some adult supervision. We also ask that, for activities which require tools or take place near water, you exercise caution and use common sense.

Activities such as wild camping and wild swimming are affected by countryside access law. You should always do your research before you set out.

Although the book is accurate at the time of going to print, some of the information may be subject to change, so please always call ahead when planning a day out to avoid disappointment. You should visit your local Wildlife Trust's website for more detail about a reserve before setting off, or call if you can't get online.

Have fun!

YOUR WILD MAP

71

113

132

SCOTLAND

NORTHERN
IRELAND

Isle of Man

NORTHUMBERLAND

TYNE &
WEAR

DURHAM

CUMBRIA

NORTH YORKSHIRE

EAST
YORKSHIRE

LANCASHIRE

WEST
YORKSHIRE

MERSEYSIDE

GREATER
MANCHESTER

SOUTH
YORKSHIRE

ANGLESEY

CONWY

FLINT

CHESHIRE

NOTTINGHAM-
SHIRE

LINCOLNSHIRE

GWYNEDD

DENBIGH

WREXHAM

DERBYSHIRE

STAFFORD-
SHIRE

SHROP-
SHIRE

POWYS

LEICESTER-
SHIRE

RUTLAND

PETERBOR.

NORFOLK

WORCESTER-
SHIRE

NORTHAMPTON-
SHIRE

CAMBRIDGE-
SHIRE

SUFFOLK

CEREDIGION

HEREFORD-
SHIRE

WARWICK-
SHIRE

BEDFORD-
SHIRE

ESSEX

PEMBROKESHIRE

CARMARTHEN-
SHIRE

MONMOUTH-
SHIRE

GLOUCESTER-

OXFORDSHIRE

BUCKINGHAM-
SHIRE

HERTFORD-
SHIRE

GREATER
LONDON

KENT

BERKSHIRE

SURREY

WILTSHIRE

HAMPSHIRE

WEST
SUSSEX

EAST
SUSSEX

SOMERSET

DEVON

DORSET

CORNWALL

50 miles

Alderney

Guernsey

CHANNEL
ISLANDS

Jersey

FRANCE

Scilly
Isles

152 WILD THINGS TO DO XI

SPRING

Spring is many people's most favourite time of year. The days gradually get lighter as the evenings extend. Buds appear, then gorgeous clusters of blossom and unfolding leaves. Spring bulbs push through warming soil. Snowdrops sparkle, followed by glorious seas of bluebells gently nodding on ancient woodland floors. Daffodils and tulips brighten up gardens. The early air is filled with birdsong, wildlife wakes up from winter, summer visitors arrive and all species prepare to procreate. Spring is all about fresh starts, new warmth and new life.

When does spring officially start? For the Met Office it all begins on 1 March, while for others the spring equinox on 20–21 March marks the start of the season. For many, though, it isn't a fixed date but nature that indicates whether or not spring has actually arrived. Traditionally the call of the cuckoo heralded the end of winter, but a recent survey by Avon Wildlife Trust revealed that many people think a chiffchaff is the ultimate sign of spring, together with

the sound of noisy great tits and the sight of bulbs bursting into bloom. The pong of wild garlic (ramsons) in woods is another popular springtime sign.

Other sights, sounds and smells that indicate it's spring include skylarks flying over farmland, wildflowers like primrose, violets and wood anemone, slow-worms sunning themselves on a garden wall, the emergence of solitary miner bees from their wintry hidey-holes and hawthorn bushes in flower. The dawn chorus is one of the loudest signs it's spring, with birds belting out classic tunes in the wee small hours from March time, in a bid to attract mates and defend territories.

Migrant birds, like swallows, swifts and house martins, return to the UK at this time of year, and pretty much all birds are nest-making by April. The arrival of warmer weather will nudge insects into action. First out will be bees, ladybirds and butterflies. Once the weather is definitely improved, damselflies will start emerging too. Amphibians will be on the move and it's at this time of year that toads embark on their hazardous walks back to breeding sites – beware of them crossing busy roads! Grass snakes, which tend to wake up at the end of March, are also worth looking out for. Though not officially wildlife, there's nothing quite like the sight of tiny lambs to tell you it is spring.

If you have a garden, it can be one of the best places to see spring arrive. Listen out for birdsong as the nesting season begins and watch out for the arrival of summer chiffchaffs and blackcaps. On warm days you may spot early butterflies, such as small tortoiseshells, making the most of the sunshine. Pondlife will also begin to stir. Keep an eye out for frogs and toads, which will arrive to mate and spawn. In no time your pond will be alive with wriggling tadpoles.

Studies show that spring is generally starting to arrive earlier, disrupting natural patterns and possibly threatening wildlife. If some animals have young earlier they may suffer from food shortages as their usual sources of sustenance may not be available. If wildlife gets out of sync, some ecologists fear the consequences could be serious. The key question is whether wildlife will be able to adapt fast enough.

Things to do in spring

- Listen to the dawn chorus
- Mulch your garden
- Grow vegetables
- Walk through a sea of bluebells
- Listen to chiffchaffs
- Climb a mountain
- Make elderflower cordial
- Create a night garden
- Start a compost heap

1.
WALK THROUGH A SEA OF BLUEBELLS

Throughout April and May, woodlands across the UK are transformed into rich-scented glades of emerald-green leaves and drooping, bell-shaped flowers. Discover a vast sea of dazzling blue hues by visiting a woodland nature reserve near you. The only thing to remember is to stick to paths when strolling through a deep bluebell sea, so you don't damage the plants.

The UK's bluebell woods are of international importance, accounting for around half of the world's total number of bluebells. It's actually illegal, under the Wildlife and Countryside Act, to dig up wild bluebell bulbs. The species is classed as endangered and dealers now face heavy fines for selling them.

Native bluebells face competition in the shape of the hybrid and the Spanish bluebell. How do you tell the difference? Natives have narrow leaves and their flowers are narrow, straight-sided bells with strongly rolled-back petals. When the weather's warm they give off a potent perfume. If the leaves are wide, the bells broad and the plant fragrance-free, you're probably dealing with a hybrid or Spanish bluebell.

Where to find a bluebell carpet

- Bunny Old Wood, Nottingham
- Castramon Wood, near Gatehouse of Fleet, Dumfries and Galloway
- Foxley Wood, near Foxley, Norfolk
- Gelli Hir Wood, near Upper Killay, Gower Penisula
- Hayley Wood, near St Neots, Cambridgeshire
- Lea and Pagets, the Wye Valley, Herefordshire
- Rigsby Wood, near Alford, Lincolnshire
- Saltburn Gill, near Redcar, Tees Valley
- Spring Wood, near Melbourne, Derbyshire
- Warburg Reserve, near Henley-on-Thames, Oxfordshire
- Warburton's Wood, near Kingsley, Cheshire

2.
SAVE THE RED SQUIRREL

With its distinctive russet fur, tufted ears and twitching tail, a red squirrel is a captivating and charming sight in the forests of the UK. Yet these flashes of red are becoming ever scarcer – the current population is estimated to be only 160,000. Scotland is an important stronghold, where it's estimated that 75% of them live, and conservationists there are working hard to restore their habitat and protect them from encroachment from grey squirrels. Red squirrel conservation efforts are also being made in areas such as mid Wales, Cumbria and Northumberland.

Grey squirrels were introduced to the UK from North America in the late 19th century and the devastating impact they've had on the native red squirrel population has been well documented. Greys have the advantage of being able to feed at ground level and digest acorns, tricks that have seen them displace their red cousins from most woodland areas. They also carry a virus that has killed many red squirrels, so it's not a good idea to encourage their presence in areas that shelter our native reds.

If you live somewhere that's still frequented by red squirrels, you could help out by getting involved with one of the many conservation projects that The Wildlife Trusts run. If you're time poor or don't have red squirrels where you live, projects always appreciate a donation, while Dorset Wildlife Trust has a squirrel adoption scheme on Brownsea Island. One of the most important things you can do is share your red squirrel sightings, as up-to-date records mean experts can accurately monitor the species' progress.

Where to see and support native reds

- Lancashire
- Anglesey
- Cumbria
- Brownsea Island
- Sefton Coast
- Isle of Mull
- Isle of Wight
- Merseyside
- Mid Wales
- Northumberland
- Scottish Borders
- Scottish Highlands
- Ulster and Eire

Red squirrel

3.
VISIT SEVENOAKS WILDLIFE RESERVE

Sevenoaks, Kent

Within easy reach of London, Sevenoaks Wildlife Reserve offers visitors a chance to get away from it all and enjoy an amazing wildlife experience whatever the time of year. With a visitor centre, shop, a mix of different wildlife habitats, including ancient woodland, reed beds and lakes, and a network of wheelchair-friendly paths, anyone can escape city life for a day and get close to the wildlife that lives here.

What will you see?

Lots! The reserve is centred around a series of lakes which were created in the 1950s from old gravel pits – the earliest example of this in the UK, and one of the first examples of collaboration between industry and a wildlife organisation.

Since its inception, a diverse array of wildlife has moved in and set up home here – over 2,000 different plants and animals have been recorded. The water levels in the lakes can be lowered or raised to create feeding and nesting areas for birds. In the winter a range of birds are attracted by the open water, including ducks like pochards, shelducks, teals, tufted ducks and shovelers that, with their big wide bills, are easy to spot from a distance.

RESERVE NAME: Sevenoaks Wildlife Reserve
GRID REF: TQ520565
NEAREST TOWN: Sevenoaks
WILDLIFE TRUST: Kent Wildlife Trust
WEBSITE: www.kentwildlifetrust.org.uk
CONTACT: 01732 456407 / info@kentwildlife.org.uk
TRANSPORT: Sevenoaks and Bat & Ball railway stations; local bus service from Sevenoaks

In the woodlands look out for woodpeckers and whitethroats. In winter tits and finches search the woods for seeds.

In the wetter areas and reed beds in spring you'll hear birds like sedge and reed warblers, back from spending the winter in Africa and marking out their breeding territory with their loud voices. Other birds you may spot around the lakes are kingfishers and sand martins. The latter can often be seen together with their larger, darker cousins, the swifts, buzzing over the water and snapping up their insect prey in mid-air.

In the summer, the lake edges abound with dragonflies and damselflies. Keep an eye out for the downy emerald dragonfly, which is nationally scarce. There are also many bees and butterflies to be found here.

Things you should know

- The reserve may look wild but don't be fooled by appearances – nearly all the wildlife habitats are man-made.
- The visitor centre houses a small museum with a fascinating collection of stuffed birds and fossils.
- There is a beautiful new sensory garden for those who are less able or with impaired vision.

'Within easy reach of London, Sevenoaks Wildlife Reserve offers visitors a chance to get away from it all'

4.
GIVE A TREE A HUG

Although, strictly speaking, trees don't really need a hug from us, they deserve one. Absorbing pollution, regulating heat in our cities, unbeatable climbing frames, homes for a wide range of wildlife, even increasing our house prices, trees really do improve our quality of life. So go on, find one near you and give it a squeeze!

5.
EXPLORE THE WEMBURY ROCK POOLS

Wembury, Devon

One of the first Voluntary Marine Conservation Areas in the UK, Wembury is a wildlife magnet. Its rocky cliffs and shoreline are home to a wide range of wildlife, while the island offshore of Wembury – the Mewstone – supports the most important colony of cormorants and shags on the south coast of England.

What will you see?

Wembury's rocky shore, slate reefs and massive wave-cut rock platforms provide one of the UK's best spots for marine plants and animals. The rock pools at Wembury are truly special and are worth a visit at any time of year, although the best time to explore them is in the spring, when animals start to return to the rock pools after spending the colder winter months further out to sea. The rock pool animals also start to breed at this time of year and visitors can find evidence of eggs and young animals in many of the pools. Even just a short time rock pooling at Wembury can be extremely rewarding, as the reserve is home to at least eight species of crab, including edible, hermit and velvet swimming crabs. Cushion starfish are a common find, as are green sea urchins and brittle starfish. Wembury is also

RESERVE NAME: Wembury Voluntary Marine Conservation Area
GRID REF: SX518484
NEAREST TOWN: Plymouth
WILDLIFE TRUST: Devon Wildlife Trust
WEBSITE: www.devonwildlifetrust.org /
www.wemburymarinecentre.org
CONTACT: 01752 802538 / info@wemburymarinecentre.org
TRANSPORT: Plymouth railway station; there is a large National Trust car park at Wembury beach
OTHER RESERVES NEARBY: Warleigh Point (SX447610), Andrew's Wood (SX707515) and Lady's Wood (SX688591)

Rockpooling at Wembury

home to the Cornish sucker fish – a rare species outside the South West – and the pipefish, which is a cousin of the sea horse and often hides under rocks or in the seaweed in the rock pools. At low tide the common blenny (or 'shanny') can be found lurking in holes above the water level, waiting for the tide to turn and the sea to come in again.

Seaweed provides food and shelter for many different animals, and there are over 100 species of seaweed at Wembury. Some of the most common are bladderwrack, kelp, sea lettuce and egg wrack, a slow-growing seaweed with large egg-shaped air bladders. Some non-native species of seaweed now grow at Wembury too, including wire weed from the Far East and harpoon weed from Australia, to name but two.

Things you should know

- Between April and September Wembury Marine Centre runs 'Rock pool Rambles' – guided tours of the rocky shore, which are open to all.
- The Marine Centre has disabled access, but access to the beach is limited and by steps only.
- Consult the local tide times before you go rock pooling and always follow the Seashore Code.
- The seaweed can get slippery, so bring sturdy footwear!
- The South West Coast Path passes directly through Wembury beach.

6. HABITATS: COASTAL AND MARINE

Think of the British seaside and lapping waves, screeching seagulls and sandcastles may spring to mind... But a whole host of wildlife calls our seas and shorelines home.

Underwater habitats like eelgrass meadows and rocky reefs are wildlife havens, home to a wide range of species, while further out to sea dolphins, sharks and whales cruise the cold oceans in search of food. Common and grey seals congregate in noisy breeding colonies every year around our coast and in some places visitors can get a really good view of these marine mammals. Magnificent seabird colonies are also dotted around the UK, home to iconic species like gannets and puffins. Other coastal habitats like estuaries and saltmarshes are also home to lots of wildlife, including rare plants and animals.

However, despite these riches currently only 0.001% of our seas are fully protected. Compare that with roughly 10% of our land area. Our seas and sea life are under threat from demand for resources like sand, gravel and oil and form overfishing and pollution. To help address this in 2009 the Marine and Coastal Access Act came into being, with the promise to create a series of Marine Conservation Zones: nationally important sites inshore and offshore. The following few years could be the most crucial period in history for the protection and management of UK seas.

The Wildlife Trusts are at the forefront of marine conservation, working and campaigning for Living Seas around the UK. As well as managing some Voluntary Marine Conservation Areas we also run marine conservation projects around the UK, collecting vital data on the state of our seas and celebrating our amazing marine wildlife. Every year we run National Marine Week in August with hundreds of family-friendly events taking place around the UK.

7.
COOK OVER A CAMPFIRE

Nothing tastes as good as piping hot food that's been cooked over your own blazing campfire as the sun sets. There are hundreds of simple ways to whip up a feast under the stars, but first you'll need to build your fire. Green wood won't burn, so divide up and hunt down a big pile of dry wood. You'll need a mixture - twigs for kindling, and bigger branches for firewood. Some campsites have their own supply of firewood, too.

Always try to use an established fire pit, to preserve the ground. If you can't find any, build your fire on rock or bare soil. Never start a fire on leaves or dry twigs, as it can easily get out of hand. If it's very windy be careful: a light breeze is fine, but if in doubt, stick to sandwiches!

1. Check if you have permission from the landowner to make a campfire.
2. Build a perimeter using large stones in a 'U' shape.
3. Lay a kindling base and light it.
4. When it's ablaze, place firewood evenly over the top.
5. When the flames have died down, add your grill – and you're ready to cook.
6. Make sure you carefully extinguish the fire before bed.
7. Don't make a campfire in an environmentally sensitive area. Nature reserves are not good places for a campfire.

8.
MAKE A WILLOW TEEPEE

Weave yourself a living tent made from rods of willow. It'll start off bare but will quickly grow its own leafy walls. Make it as big or as small as you like, depending on how much space and how much willow you have. Source willow rods from a garden centre or a specialist supplier, or use trimmings from your own willow tree.

Or just get creative with your willow and weave any of kind of structure you like. Plant your teepee well away from buildings and drains.

You will need ...

- Long rods of willow – some thick and some thinner
- Chalk
- A large hammer
- Strong string or flexible rubber ties

How to do it

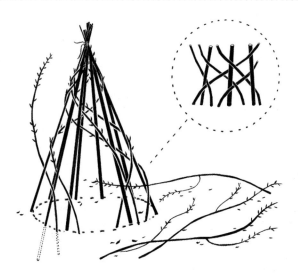

1. Use chalk or rope to mark a circle on the ground that's as big as you want the circumference of your teepee to be.
2. Plant evenly spaced thick willow rods around the edge of the circle, pushing them 30 cm deep into the ground so they can establish solid roots. If the ground is hard make a hole first, using a hammer and something like a stake.
3. Plant the thinner willow rods in the spaces between the thick ones, weaving them all to the left, so the bottom of the thin rod crosses its thicker left-hand neighbour and the top of it crosses its left-hand next-door neighbour but one.
4. Then plant more thin rods, this time weaving them all to the right.
5. Securely tie up the point at the top where all the willow rods meet.
6. You have a finished teepee structure, which should start to sprout soon.

9.
SPOT WILD DAFFODILS
IN WALLIS WOOD

Ockley, Surrey

What will you see?

Semi-natural woodland that can be traced back to Neolithic times, Wallis Wood is a typical example of Weald Clay hazel coppice woodland. Cut through by an attractive stream, it also has a small pool and surrounding pasture. The coppiced woodland is of different ages and is cut on a rotational basis, which allows a rich ground flora to develop, including carpets of bluebells, broad-leaved violet and violet helleborine orchids, common spotted orchids, primroses, wood anemone and wood sorrel. Make sure you look out for the rare wild daffodil which is restricted in Surrey to the woods on the Weald Clay. Both species of British oak are present together with ash, hornbeam, Midlands hawthorn, wild apple, wild cherry and wild service tree.

The reserve supports a variety of rare woodland butterflies, including purple emperors, purple hairstreaks, silver-washed fritillaries, white admirals and speckled woods. A particular rarity of the site is the triangle spider (*Hyptiotes paradoxus*), which makes its home in yew trees and is only recorded in one other site in Surrey.

A number of typical woodland birds can be found on the reserve, including five species of tit and several spring migrants. Dormice have also been recorded on the site and, together with the ongoing coppicing regime, management of the site is targeted at protecting the valuable wildlife habitat that exists here. It's well worth a visit and two other Trust reserves are under four miles away too.

Things you should know

- Access to the site is via paths and tracks.
- In wet weather the ground can get very sticky because of the clay, so make sure you wear suitable footwear.

RESERVE NAME: Wallis Wood
GRID REF: TQ121388
NEAREST TOWN: Ockley
WILDLIFE TRUST: Surrey Wildlife Trust
WEBSITE: www.surreywildlifetrust.co.uk
CONTACT: 01483 795440 / info@surreywt.org.uk
TRANSPORT: Limited parking on site
OTHER RESERVES: Vann Lake (TQ157394) and Fowls Copse (TQ067418). Please contact the Trust for a permit to visit these reserves

10.
GROW VEGETABLES

Reduce food miles and adopt more seasonal and sustainable eating habits by growing your own wildlife-friendly, organic veg. Certain fruits and vegetables have particularly good wildlife credentials, catering for both you and the wildlife around you. Bees' needs especially must be taken into account. These precious pollinators need all the help they can get after recent population crashes and they're essential visitors if you want a successful kitchen garden.

The flowers on many fruit and vegetable crops are firm favourites of bees – beans, peas and fragrant herbs are loved, as are apples, currants and raspberries. If you have space in or around your vegetable plot, include flowers like bluebells, forget-me-nots, foxgloves, lupins and primroses to lure in pollinators.

Grow beans

Runner beans are one of the easiest crops in the world to grow. With a little love and attention they will attain impressive heights and come summer be covered in flowers that bees absolutely love. You will be rewarded with handsome crops of delicious runners well into early autumn if the weather's mild. All you need is a flower bed or a large container filled with organic, peat-free compost, plus some canes or a wall for the beans to grow against. They don't grow well in the same spot so you'll need to move them each year or change the soil for best results.

Practise companion planting

Companion planting is a traditional method of growing different plants together for mutual benefits, like extra nutrients, protection from harsh weather and pest control. For example, nasturtiums grown among your brassicas will protect them from caterpillars, as the caterpillars may choose to eat the nasturtium leaves rather than your cabbages. Chives or sage among your carrots may ward off aphids, while garlic may deter them from your roses and chervil will keep them off your lettuces. You can use plants like limanthes (the poached egg plant) to attract hoverflies which predate on aphids.

Small-scale growing

If you don't have a garden, you can grow herbs, tumbling tomatoes, strawberries and many varieties of lettuce and salad leaves in a window box or hanging basket, all of which will be happy growing both inside and out.

11.
WATCH SUNSET

This is easy, though it requires a little luck. Just make sure you're outside on a clear evening and hope for something stunning.

Sunsets can be magnificent in cities as well as on hilltops. The accidental view from the top of a double-decker bus can be jaw-dropping every once in a while.

In winter, sunset comes early and feels more important, washing the sky with much-needed colour for a few glorious moments amid the gloom. The sky somehow seems bigger in the winter too, when the trees are bare and the air is icy.

The best sunsets are probably the ones that happen while you're on holiday, when you're relaxed and you can watch it from start to finish in all its burning glory. Watching the sun pool and drop into a lake or ocean is truly joyful and often memorable.

12.
VISIT A CAVE

It's always exciting to visit a cave, especially if it's a really dark and drippy one, full of mirror pools, stalactites and stalagmites. Despite a lack of light, caves can host a variety of wildlife, including fungi, invertebrates and mammals.

Things like fungus gnats, drone flies, caddis flies and crane flies can be found in caves, as can tissue and herald moths. Peacock, small tortoiseshell and comma butterflies sometimes hibernate in cave thresholds. The European cave spider obviously loves dark caverns, while foxes have been known to frequent them. Coastal caves provide shelter for many sea creatures. And of course, caves are important habitats for many species of bat, especially during periods of hibernation.

You need a permit and a hard hat to visit Devon Wildlife Trust's Higher Kiln Quarry reserve, but it's well worth it. Some of the caves preserve a fascinating record of the mammals that lived in Devon during the Pleistocene era, an ice age that ended over 100,000 years ago. The Joint Mitnor Cave (part of the complex at Higher Kiln) contains the richest assemblage of mammal remains in Britain, preserving animals that migrated northwards from continental Europe as the glaciers retreated. Elephants, rhinoceroses, bears, hyenas, cave lions and giant deer are among the 18 different species that fell to their deaths down an open shaft into the cave. The caves at Higher Kiln are now an important winter roost site for rare horseshoe bats.

 A few more cave sites

- Blackhall Rocks, Durham
- Brown's Folly, Gloucester
- Cheddar Gorge and Caves, Somerset
- Dan-yr-Ogof Caves, South Wales
- Thor's Cave, Derbyshire
- Hill of White Hamars, Orkney
- King Arthur's Cave, Herefordshire
- Long Hole Cliff, Glamorgan
- Marble Arch Caves, County Fermanagh
- Gaping Gill, North Yorshire

13.
COOK NETTLE SOUP

Healthy, delicious and found absolutely everywhere, nettles are a wonder leaf that can be cooked up into a wholesome soup. Food that's free and full of goodness – perfect! You'll need to pick the tender tops of young nettles in the spring.

You will need ...

- 450 g young nettle tops
- 8 wild garlic (ramson) leaves, torn (optional)
- 4 medium potatoes, peeled and chopped
- 4 shallots, chopped
- 2 celery sticks, chopped
- 50 g butter
- 1 litre vegetable stock

'Food that's free and full of goodness – perfect!'

How to do it

1. Go nettle picking – make sure you wear gloves and long sleeves!
2. Boil the potatoes until tender, then drain.
3. Melt the butter in a large pan and cook the shallots, celery and wild garlic leaves over a low heat with a lid for 10 minutes until soft but not brown.
4. Wearing rubber gloves, sort through the nettles, selecting new, young tops and discarding any tough stalks.
5. Blanch the nettles in boiling water for 2–3 minutes.
6. Add the stock, cooked potatoes and blanched nettles to the pan. Simmer for 5–10 minutes, until the nettles are tender.
7. Purée in a blender then return to the pan and reheat. Season well.
8. You could stir in some crème fraiche or serve with a swirl of cream and some crusty bread.

14.
DISCOVER THE WILD SIDE OF THE MENDIPS

Black Rock, Somerset

Black Rock Nature Reserve is one of a network of linked Somerset Wildlife Trust reserves on the slopes of the Mendip Hills around Cheddar Gorge. It has a diverse mix of habitats and spectacular views south across the Somerset Levels.

What will you see?

The site's limestone grassland is testament to the reserve's status as a wildlife hotspot. Over 30 species of plant have been recorded here per square metre, including the scarce spring cinquefoil. In the summer these areas are great for butterfly watching and there is a chance of seeing uncommon species like the dark green fritillary, dingy skipper and green hairstreak, all of which have been recorded here.

Meanwhile, the rocky outcrops, cliffs and screes, characteristic of the Cheddar Gorge landscape, are home to rare plant species such as angular Solomon's-seal, limestone fern and Cheddar bedstraw, the latter being endemic to the Cheddar area. The coppice woodland on the reserve is home to lots of wildlife including rare mammals like dormouse and yellow-necked mouse, both of which use nest boxes provided by the Trust. Badger setts occur throughout the reserve and both greater and lesser horseshoe bats use the reserve for feeding. At the top of Black Rock you can enjoy sprawling views across Cheddar Gorge and look out for peregrine falcons hunting over the reserve.

Adders and grass snakes can both be found at Black Rock, along with a wide range of birds including redstart, yellowhammer and whitethroat. For dedicated slug and snail hunters the site boasts a variety of molluscs including the nationally scarce large chrysalis snail and the ash-black slug – a species restricted in Somerset to Mendip and Exmoor.

Black Rock is close to several other Somerset Wildlife Trust nature reserves so you can easily spend a day exploring. Spring is a great time to visit nearby Longwood reserve, where thousands of bluebells create a haze of blue on the woodland floor.

Things you should know

- The reserve is open all year round, and there are well-marked footpaths and nature trails.
- There is an abandoned quarry on the reserve, and sometimes there can be rock falls – so beware!

RESERVE NAME: Black Rock
GRID REF: ST483544
NEAREST TOWN: Cheddar
WILDLIFE TRUST: Somerset Wildlife Trust
WEBSITE: www.somersetwildlife.org
CONTACT: 01823 652400/ enquiries@somersetwildlife.org
TRANSPORT: The site lies on either side of the B3135; excellent bus routes serve the area

15.
RACE SNAILS

The first rule of snail racing is: be kind to the snails. First make a snail-racing track. Draw a large circle with a radius of 33 cm and mark the centre with a smaller circle. This smaller circle will be your starting line – snails race from the centre to the edge of the large circle. A white board or cloth can make a good racetrack. Collect some snails from your garden or local park – look behind and underneath big stones, and in damp areas. Gather some willing snail racers, each select a snail and mark them carefully and gently with stickers, perhaps using numbers or colours to distinguish them. Then nominate a snail trainer, whose job it is to keep the course watered throughout the race because snails like damp conditions.

It's time to line the snails up along the edge of the central circle, facing outwards. The snail trainer shouts, 'Ready, steady, SLOW!' and they're off. The winner is the first snail to reach the edge of the outer circle. Remember to put your snails back where you found them.

The world record stands at 2 minutes over the 33 cm, set in 1995 by a snail called Archie. The World Snail-Racing Championships are held every year at Congham near King's Lynn in Norfolk.

16.
LEARN BIRD CALLS

Birds both call and sing. Calls are usually shorter, sharper and more urgent, used to sound an alarm or maintain contact with a flock. Song tends to come from male birds and is longer and sweeter, used to attract mates and defend territories. Not all birds have a song, but many do and the best time to hear them in action is at dawn in springtime.

Birdsong and calls are incredibly useful to birdwatchers, helping them to both locate birds and identify them. It's worth swotting up as sometimes a bird's call or song can be its most distinguishing feature, the one thing that differentiates two species that otherwise look almost identical. One of the best ways to learn birdsongs is to listen to recordings of them. You can buy CDs of songs or find free recordings online – both are invaluable tools.

 Birds to listen out for

BLACKBIRD: Call is a loud 'chik, chik, chik'; song is slow, with melodic flute-like tones.

CHAFFINCH: Call is 'pink pink' and 'chip chip'; song is enthusiastic and repetitive.

STARLING: Call is 'tsiew' or 'tcherr'; song is a series of whistles and mimicry.

GREAT TIT: Call is a constant chattering 'tsee-tsee'; song is a wheezy 'tea-cher, tea-cher'.

ROBIN: Call is a sharp 'tic' and 'tseee'; song is confident and powerful in spring, wistful and melancholic in winter, without repetition.

SONG THRUSH: Call is a single 'tsip' or 'chick chick'; song is repetitive, with fluting phrases.

SWALLOW: Call is 'tswit tswit'; song is an enthusiastic twitter.

DUNNOCK: Call is a high-pitched 'chik-chik'; song is a short repeated warble.

WILLOW WARBLER: Call is 'who-eet' and 'pew pew'; song is lyrical and falling.

WREN: Call is a loud 'chik' and 'chur'; song is a loud, rattling, fast paced staccato.

Robin

Wren

An osprey at
Rutland Water

17.
ENJOY AN OSPREY CRUISE
AT RUTLAND WATER

Oakham, Rutland

A visit to Rutland Water, a huge reservoir nestled amid the rolling countryside of England's smallest county, is a chance to enjoy fine views and some excellent wildlife watching. Visit in summer for the opportunity to see southern England's only breeding ospreys.

What will you see?

Ospreys are spectacular fish-eating birds of prey that spend the winter in tropical West Africa before migrating north to nest and breed. Ospreys have been breeding at Rutland Water since 2001, following a successful reintroduction project. The reservoir is now one of the best places in the UK to watch these magnificent birds from late March to early September.

One of the most exciting ways of seeing ospreys at Rutland Water is to take a guided boat trip with members of the Rutland Osprey Project

'Rutland Water is the place to go if you want to see an osprey'

Team aboard the Rutland Belle. The idea is simple – the boat sails to the parts of the reservoir where ospreys are regularly seen fishing and, with a bit of luck, those on board are able to enjoy spectacular close-up views of the birds as they dive for fish. If you have seen a hunting osprey in action, you will know this is something not to be missed!

Even on those rare occasions when the ospreys prove elusive, there's always a good range of the reservoir's other wildlife on view and high-lights often include Arctic terns in spring and red kites throughout the summer. There's also every chance of hearing singing nightingales as the boat sails past woodland where these magical songsters breed.

Each cruise begins with refreshments and an introductory talk at the Anglian Water Bird-watching Centre, giving you the full lowdown on the project and the birds.

Things you should know

- Rutland Water Nature Reserve is situated at Egleton on the west shore of Rutland Water and at Lyndon on the south shore. There are numerous trails, paths and bird-watching hides allowing excellent views over the reserve.
- Tickets for the Osprey Cruises allow access to the nature reserve and Whitwell car park, otherwise car park charges apply to Rutland Water.
- You can cycle around the reservoir and there are bike hire facilities locally.

RESERVE NAME: Rutland Water Nature Reserve
GRID REF: SK878075 (Egleton) and SK894058 (Lyndon)
NEAREST TOWN: Oakham
WILDLIFE TRUST: Leicestershire and Rutland Wildlife Trust
WEBSITE: www.lrwt.org.uk / www.rutlandwater.org.uk
CONTACT: 0116 2720444 / info@lrwt.org.uk
Contact the Osprey Team to book an Osprey Cruise on
01572 737 378 / tmackrill@lrwt.org.uk
TRANSPORT: Oakham railway station; parking on site

18.
CLIMB A MOUNTAIN

The tough ascent and anticipation, the pause and breathtaking view, the jolting descent and sense of achievement – climbing mountains is hard work but very rewarding. Eyeing the towering mass before you set out is daunting, but looking back at it after it's been conquered is pure pleasure. The UK has some superbly hilly areas, with climbs ranging from easy to super difficult. All you need for the simpler climbs is decent weather, good boots, a map, a compass and a first-aid kit. And perhaps a secret stash of sweets for extra energy.

What kinds of wildlife can survive in the sometimes extremely inhospitable climes of a mountainside? As well as offering jagged, sweeping vistas of crags, dips, rocks and valleys, mountains are great places to spot plants like hardy alpines, mosses and heathers, which can set slopes ablaze with colour at certain times of year.

Species like alpine clubmoss, alpine gentian, map lichen, mountain avens, mossy saxifrage and purple saxifrage all thrive on hillsides, providing homes for mountain-loving invertebrates. In Snowdonia you could see birds such as ravens, peregrine falcons, ring ouzels, meadow pipits and wheatears. In the uplands of Scotland you might chance upon a graceful mountain hare, which sports a snow-white coat in winter, or, if you are very lucky, a golden eagle.

Mountainous regions to explore

- The Brecon Beacons
- The Cambrians
- The Cairngorms
- The Grampians
- The Lake District
- The Mourne Mountains
- The Peak District
- Snowdonia

The three peaks

- **SCAFELL PIKE** (978 m) – Lake District National Park, Cumbria
- **SNOWDON** (1,085 m) – Snowdonia National Park, Gwynedd
- **BEN NEVIS** (1,334 m) – Lochaber, Scottish Highlands

'The UK has some superbly hilly areas, with climbs ranging from easy to super difficult'

Snowdon

Pink-footed geese

19.
GO MIGRATION WATCHING

The seasonal and often epic journeys undertaken by many species of bird can make for some spine-tingling bird watching. Migration usually occurs in response to weather and habitat conditions or food availability, and follows seasonal patterns that mean it's possible to time your twitching to coincide with mass bird movements.

Spring and autumn are the peak migration periods and journeys happen at night as well as during the day. Changing migration patterns are key indicators of shifts in ecosystems and can, for example, help scientists monitor global issues like climate change. It's believed that migrating birds navigate by three compasses, using the sun, the stars and the earth's magnetic field to keep them on course.

Spring

Look out for swallows, house martins, swifts, willow warblers, chiffchaffs, flycatchers, wheatears, redstarts, nightingales, yellow wagtails, tree pipits, cuckoos, nightjars, turtle doves, hobbies, ospreys, terns and Manx shearwaters arriving from the Mediterranean and Africa. Seabirds like puffins and gannets head back to land at this time of year too, after spending the winter out at sea. Spring visitors come to the insect-rich UK to breed before heading south again, come autumn.

Autumn

Visitors head here from the north and east to spend the winter in the UK, where the weather is milder and food is easier to find. Some blackbirds and starlings are in fact winter visitors from Eastern Europe, and these mingle with our resident populations. You might see or hear fieldfares and redwings or wading birds like curlew, lapwing, oystercatcher and redshank on the move in autumn. Whooper and Bewick swans and several species of geese also head to the UK in large flocks at this time of year. Many water birds also spend the winter on the sea around the UK coast, including common scoters and great northern divers. Come spring, these species will head back to their northern breeding grounds.

'Migrating birds navigate by three compasses, using the sun, the stars and the earth's magnetic field'

20.
START A COMPOST HEAP

Composting is the oldest method of recycling. It's a great way of turning green waste (see overleaf for examples) into rich, crumbly compost for your garden or allotment. You can make your compost heap on the ground or you could build or buy a box. A container will help to keep the heap dry, warm and tidy. Place it somewhere it will stay moist, but not wet – shady spots are good – and to allow air to circulate throughout. Make a base from two rows of bricks covered with sticks and twigs.

To start it off you could stockpile green waste for a week or two and then build a heap, or just start from scratch building up as you go. Mix a variety of materials together. Avoid putting too many rough stems and twigs in the mix as they are slow to break down. Grass cuttings are useful, but mix them in well with leaves, kitchen waste and stems to prevent things getting sloppy. Adding layers of shredded paper and » cardboard can also help combat too much moisture. Firm down the heap, but don't squash it completely as you want to leave small air spaces in it. Extra waste can be added as the heap sinks down.

Cover the heap with a bit of old carpet or a sheet of polythene – this helps it stay warm and keeps the rain out. If it gets too wet it may start to smell.

Compost is ready to use when all the ingredients have turned into a dark crumbly mixture with an earthy smell. Turning once or twice can speed the process up and help to ensure everything gets a go in the middle of the pile. It may take a few months until your compost is ready but it is worth the wait! Dig it into your garden soil to refresh its structure and replace lost nutrients. Spread it around plants to keep moisture in the soil, protect from frost and stop weeds growing.

Lots of councils have schemes where you can buy cheap compost bins, so it's worth checking to see if your local council has any.

'Dig compost into your garden soil to refresh its structure and replace lost nutrients'

Recipe for good compost

- Annual weeds
- Grass cuttings
- Pet hair
- Shredded paper
- Horse manure
- Leaves
- Wet straw and hay
- Vegetable and fruit peelings
- Tea leaves and coffee grounds
- Flowers

Not good for composting

- Meat
- Fish
- Dairy products
- Cooked food
- Cat litter
- Nappies
- Coal ash
- Perennial weeds

21.
HABITATS: PARKLAND

Parkland can be the grand, sweeping estates of historic country houses, or the more humble setting of local urban parks, complete with playground and football field. As well as being of historic and cultural importance, parks can also provide habitats for all kinds of wildlife such as foxes, bats, birds, butterflies, bees, mosses and lichens.

Some of the most famous UK parklands are managed by the Royal Parks in London. Richmond Park is the largest, covering over 1,000 hectares (that's roughly the size of 2,000 football pitches!), hosting 650 roaming deer and more than 1,000 kinds of beetle. As a Site of Special Scientific Interest and a National Nature Reserve, it's been nationally recognised for its wildlife value. But it's not just large parklands that are good for wildlife. Every patch of green space is important as we try to link up our isolated nature reserves with the wider landscape, and in urban areas parks and gardens can be vital refuges or 'stepping stones' for wildlife.

Created by people for people, parks are often places for picnics, ball games, reading a book or going for a jog. So a well-maintained local park can provide both an urban wildlife haven and a much-needed part of a community. They also give us the chance to watch wildlife from common ducks and swans, to rarer bats and newts.

Parkland does face some significant issues such as isolation through surrounding development and pollution from traffic and fertilisers. To help those managing our parklands, The Wildlife Trusts offer advice on many subjects from putting up nest boxes for birds to growing glorious wildflower meadows alongside manicured lawns.

Painted lady
butterfly

22.
FEED BUTTERFLIES

Many species of butterfly have suffered due to the loss of wildflower meadows, hedgerows and woodland. Pesticide and herbicide sprays have also had a negative impact on butterfly populations. With a bit of thought and some careful planning, you can help butterflies by providing food sources in your garden.

Attract them with nectar-rich flowers, choosing plants with simple flowers that make it easy for butterflies to access the nectar. Avoid double-flowered varieties as they often have no nectar. Plant them in a sheltered, sunny spot and don't forget to provide food plants for caterpillars too. Aubretia, primrose, sweet rocket, valerian, marjoram, lavender, knapweed, globe thistle, verbena, sweet scabious, ice plant and Michaelmas daisy are all good.

You could also make a butterfly feeder to provide them with an extra boost. This could be a lifesaver if butterflies are tempted out of hibernation on a mild winter day. Fluttering about at the wrong time of year, when nectar supplies are low, steals valuable energy supplies from them and they could die. Some sugary water helps keep them going. A dish of sugar water would do, or you could get a bit more creative...

You will need ...

- Card
- A plastic bottle top
- A straw
- Tape
- A pot with soil
- Cotton wool
- Sugar
- Water

How to make your butterfly feeder

1. Draw a flower on your card and colour it in with bright colours, then cut it out.
2. Stick a plastic bottle top in the centre of the flower.
3. Tape the straw on to the back of the flower and stand it in the pot of soil.
4. Mix the sugar with some water and soak the cotton wool in the solution.
5. Put the cotton wool inside the bottle top.
6. Place your feeder outside, somewhere sunny on a warm day.

23.
MAKE A SOLITARY-BEE HOME

There are over 200 species of solitary bee in the UK, and their nests are usually tunnels in which the bee builds a series of chambers to hold a fertilised egg and store a pollen-rich food supply for the developing larvae. A solitary-bee home is easy to make, lasts for years and can provide a welcome home for bees in your garden.

Take a substantial piece of dry timber, like an old gate post, at least 15cm square, place it in a sunny, sheltered spot and fix it firmly into the ground, so that about a metre is visible. Using an extra-long drill bit, and angling the drill slightly upwards, drill holes in a random pattern into the wood in diameters ranging from 2 mm (lots) to 8 mm (just a few). The slight angle will allow the holes to drain.

Nail a roof on top to keep the rain off and try to maintain a muddy puddle nearby as bees use mud to build their brood chambers. Note that bees don't like the smell of freshly cut wood so you'll need to wait for it to weather a bit before any move in.

24.
GO CLOUDSPOTTING

Cloudspotting has to be one of the cheapest, and most addictive, hobbies. Once you start watching the skies it's hard to stop. Predicting the weather, admiring a particularly fine example of a nimbostratus or maybe just spotting strange shapes in the sky, you may find yourself looking upwards at any opportunity.

Clouds are grouped and named in the same way as plants and animals. This means they are divided into groups called genera, species and varieties. Throughout our atmosphere, there are 10 main types of cloud, which can be broken up into many smaller species and varieties. Here are some of the most common clouds to look out for:

Cumulus

This cloud often looks like a fluffy splodge of cotton wool in the sky. Cumulus clouds have flat bases and cauliflower-shaped tops. They appear on sunny days, at the top of invisible columns of hot air rising up from the ground. (Pictured)

Cumulonimbus

Cumulonimbus are little fluffy cumulus clouds grown out of control! They can reach an enormous size, up to several miles in height. They are the only clouds powerful enough to produce thunder and lightning. If you are a long way from a cumulonimbus and see an anvil shape at the top, this is called an incus. It can spread over hundreds of miles across the sky, and spells bad weather!

Cirrus

These clouds form up to 8 miles above our heads and look like giant wispy horse tails. They are often seen on really clear, bright days. The bad news is that if you can see more cirrus clouds forming, a nimbostratus is probably heading your way (see below). The wispy bits are a "rain" of ice crystals falling through the atmosphere. They are called "fallstreaks".

Nimbostratus

Bad luck if you are standing under one of these. It is a low cloud which is full to bursting with water, and this water will fall on our heads as rain, sleet or snow. A nimbostratus cloud can rain for hours and hours and hours.

Fog or mist

Fog and mist are clouds that have formed around us at ground level. You are more likely to see them after cold, clear nights when warm air gets cold very quickly and the water vapour turns to droplets before it has a chance to rise high in the sky. The difference between a fog and mist is the thickness of the cloud.

25.
WATCH A SPIDER
SPIN A WEB

It's one of the wonders of the natural world and it happens all around you. Watching a spider spin a web, starting with just a single, apparently flimsy, strand of silk, is a nature-watching experience that can rival any other.

Spiders weave their webs from silk that they produce from a gland in their abdomen. It's liquid when it leaves the spider's body but dries and turns solid when it meets the air. Spiders create different kinds of silk for different uses such as catching insects or building cocoons. Different spiders make different shaped webs.

Autumn is good time to see spiders but you can find them almost everywhere, inside and out and almost all year round.

Try filming a spider spinning a web using a digital camera and a small tripod or other flat surface for support. This will give you a fixed position to film from, and will hold the camera steady while the spider does its work. Then speed up the end result to get your very own mini nature film.

26.
TAKE A WANDER THROUGH MAGICAL WOODS

Woolhope, Herefordshire

Wessington Pasture is a magical place for children to safely explore without getting lost. With a mixture of hillside pasture, new and established woodland and a pond, it's the perfect place to let your children play wild, build dens and get close to nature.

What will you see?

Wessington has a loop walk which is easy to stick to, but there are plenty of choices for adventurers to make along the way. Wander around where the old trees grow and feel the woodland magic. Can you find the tree that looks like a castle? Or the fallen tree that looks like a dinosaur skeleton? Fallen trees are great to climb on, but test their branches first to avoid a tumble!

'Wessington Pasture is the perfect place to let your children play wild'

As you wander through the woods look out for signs of the creatures that live here. You might see badger setts or rabbit holes and if you are particularly lucky (and quiet) you might even see a deer! In the meadow look out for little round holes made in the long grass by mice.

Perhaps you could build a den to camouflage yourself? At the top of the reserve there are some great trees that have fallen or grown in a big bend - the beginning of a great den. You just need to collect large branches to fill in the gaps. Don't use anything living to make your den - there are plenty of fallen branches available, especially in the new woodland area. Because of the brambles and blackthorn trees it might be a good idea to wear gardening gloves (you can buy child-sized ones online) while you are den building since thorns and spikes in fingers are never fun.

When you can, look around you at the surrounding hills. If you have a map and compass you can use these to identify what's around you.

Den building at Wessington

Try to spot May Hill in Gloucestershire with its little crown of trees on top. There is also Caplor Camp, Lea and Pagets Wood to see on the horizon. Can you find them?

Finish off your visit with a rest in the bird hide. There's a journal to record your visit and most importantly, what you have seen. Leave a message for the Trust or draw a picture of something you've seen.

Things you should know

- The reserve is most suited to children over five years old, as there are some steep, muddy paths that are not pushchair-friendly.
- In autumn and winter it can get pretty muddy so don't forget your wellies!

RESERVE NAME: Wessington Pasture
GRID REF: SO605354
NEAREST TOWN: Hereford
WILDLIFE TRUST: Herefordshire Nature Trust
WEBSITE: www.herefordshirewt.org
CONTACT: 01432 356872 / email via the website
TRANSPORT: Take the B224 from Hereford; parking on site

Basking shark in Manx waters

27.
SEA-WATCHING ON
THE ISLE OF MAN

Ayres Visitor Centre, Manx

Ayres Visitor Centre lies within a wildlife-rich stretch of low-lying sand dune coastline, stretching for five miles from Cronk-y-Bing to the Point of Ayre at the northern tip of the Isle of Man.

What will you see?

The Manx Wildlife Trust has established a Visitor Centre and Nature Trail here to increase public understanding of this vulnerable and wildlife-rich area and to provide information about its birds, natural habitats and rare plants. The Nature Trail leads the visitor from the shingle beach through the marram sand dunes and onto the expanse of heath.

Moving inland, marram grass and other plants colonise the upper shore area. Dotted amongst the sand dunes are spectacular displays of burnet rose, pyramidal orchids and many other plants and insects. Further inland again is the heath, with its rare lichens, nesting stonechats, oystercatchers and lapwings and busy insect populations.

The Ayres Visitor Centre is also the perfect location for a spot of sea watching, as it sits at the northern tip of the Isle of Man, a handy travel route for marine mammals, basking sharks and other megafauna as they make their way between coastlines. Sea-watching from the shore can be very rewarding, with diving gannets and terns often seen off-shore in summer, and an impressive list of seabirds and waders at any season. Twelve species of whales and dolphins have been recorded in Manx waters over the last few years. Three of these are seen very regularly – Harbour porpoise, Risso's dolphin and Minke whale. Harbour porpoises are found all round the island and are easier to see when the sea is flat calm. Other species that are seen fairly frequently are the bottlenose dolphin, the common dolphin and the mighty killer whale. Grey seals are also a common sight at Ayres.

In summer the waters of the Isle of Man are home to one of the world's largest concentrations of basking sharks. They are found all round the Island but are more frequently sighted off the west coast. The numbers seen vary widely from year to year, and it is often possible to see them from the shore.

You should know

- This stunning area is at risk from damage caused by fire, vehicles and dogs, so it's really important that visitors pay attention to the Country Code.
- You can go on boat trips to watch marine wildlife. Always use a WiSe accredited operator. Details can be found on the WiSe website or from the Isle of Man tourism office.

RESERVE NAME: Ayres Visitor Centre
GRID REF: NX435038
NEAREST TOWN: Bride
WILDLIFE TRUST: Manx Wildlife Trust
WEBSITE: www.manxwt.org.uk
CONTACT: 01624 801985/ enquiries@manxwt.org.uk
TRANSPORT: The Visitor Centre is signposted on the Ballaghennie Road, west of Bride

28.
VISIT SILENT VALLEY LOCAL NATURE RESERVE

Silent Valley, Gwent

The past 300 years have been a time of great change for the Gwent Valleys. Nowhere can this change be seen more clearly than at the Silent Valley Local Nature Reserve, where wildlife is taking over but signs of the site's mining past are still visible today.

What will you see?

Much of the Silent Valley is open woodland, dotted with areas that were once meadows. Further up the hillside is an old tramline, locally called a Dramline. It used to take coal from the levels bored straight into the hillside. The mining spoil is colonised by mosses and liverworts. Nature is reclaiming an old coal tip with lichens, mosses, heather, grasses and, in the wetter areas, alder trees. Cones from the alder tree form a valuable food supply for birds like siskins, redpolls and tits.

'If you're after a challenging ramble in the untamed countryside, the trails of Silent Valley could be for you'

The reserve is known for its wet flushes, areas of wetter ground which are ideal for plants like marsh thistle, wood horsetail – which looks like a mini Christmas tree – and marsh violets. The latter two plants can be easily seen from the lower woodland paths. Lichens, ferns and mosses also grow throughout the reserve. Small pearl bordered fritillary butterflies can also be seen on the reserve and their caterpillars feast on the abundant violets in the reserve. These butterflies are in worrying decline across the UK and in many places their local populations are clinging on, relying on safe areas of habitat in nature reserves like Silent Valley. Down in the lower meadows you will find ant nests and sometimes green woodpeckers feeding on the ants.

LEFT TO RIGHT
Silent Valley • Brambling

If you're after a challenging ramble in the untamed countryside, the trails of Silent Valley could be for you. The steep inclines of rocky pathways are worth negotiating as you make your way to the UK's highest and most westerly Beech woodland, home to an array of plants and animals that rely on this precious habitat. Beech trees provide a large supply of beech nuts, used for food by winter flocks of chaffinches and bramblings. Other birds that you might find nesting in the woodlands include the pied flycatcher and redstart.

You should know

- There are well-maintained paths around the reserve, but some are very steep in places and they can get muddy.

RESERVE NAME: Silent Valley
GRID REF: SO187 062
NEAREST TOWN: Cwm
WILDLIFE TRUST: Gwent Wildlife Trust
WEBSITE: www.gwentwildlife.org
CONTACT: 01600 740600 / info@gwentwildlife.org
TRANSPORT: The Reserve is at the top of Cendl Terrace in Cwm

29.
HABITATS: MEADOW

A perfect picture of the countryside, rolling meadows filled with wild flowers are actually actively managed grasslands. Unimproved by fertilisers, these meadows are cut for hay in late summer and after the summer profusion of colourful flowers. The flowering plants set seed before the hay is cut and the meadow is grazed in late summer and autumn.

Among the most common grasses found in meadows are Yorkshire fog, smooth meadow grass, crested dog's tail, sweet vernal grass and red fescue. These are accompanied by the purples, pinks, whites and yellows of herbs like devil's-bit scabious, pepper saxifrage, ox-eye daisy, black knapweed and buttercups. In damper areas, sneezewort, lady's smock, ragged-robin, meadow sweet and yellow iris can be found, as well as rarer species like narrow-leaved water dropwort.

Walking through a peaceful meadow, your head filled with the scent of wild flowers, is a magical experience, and one chock-full of wildlife. The hedgerows, bright with spring blossom, provide excellent nesting and feeding sites for birds such as chiffchaff and yellowhammer. Delicate gatekeeper and holly blue butterflies flutter through the grasses, kestrels hover overhead, badgers make tracks through the grasses and ditches provide shelter for frogs and mice.

But in recent years, over 95% of our wildflower meadows have disappeared, lost to drainage and development. Without care, those meadows that are left can quickly become overgrown as grasses shade out delicate flowers and brambles take over. So The Wildlife Trusts are working to prevent further loss by looking after many meadows as nature reserves where traditional management techniques, such as hay-cutting, reseeding and grazing, help them to continue their colourful yearly cycle.

Blackbird – a familiar sound
in the dawn chorus

30.
LISTEN TO THE
DAWN CHORUS

It tends to start in early March, reaching a crescendo in April and May. It's not restricted to UK wildernesses, but echoes through our towns and cities as well as the countryside. The spring dawn chorus is an auditory spectacle that is impossible to miss. It will be cold and dark outside but the air will ring with birdsong, a natural roar that's reminiscent of being in the jungle rather than the suburbs.

Most of the birds that sing are male and they do so to defend their territory and attract a mate. Blackbirds, robins or skylarks usually start things off, followed perhaps by song thrushes and wrens. The chorus begins in earnest as the sun rises, around 5am in late April and early May, by which time the UK's resident songbirds are joined by summer visitors like blackcaps and willow warblers.

At dawn the air is calm and other noises are low. Birdsong travels further and has more impact. Studies suggest that a dawn song is 20 times more effective than one belted out at midday. Female birds tend to lay eggs in the morning, so it makes sense for males to attempt to attract mates just before. The chorus of song also reveals which birds are perching where, and whether any territories have become vacant overnight.

The best time to hear it is the first hour before sunrise – which means getting up early or staying up really late. Wildlife Trusts around the UK always organise special events to celebrate International Dawn Chorus Day on the first Sunday in May, but if you can't make it along to an event, set your alarm, open a window and let the dawn chorus spill in over your duvet.

31.
CREATE A NIGHT GARDEN

Gardens are wonderful places as dusk rolls in, colours bleach out and the air fills with night noises. Indulging in an alfresco drink on a balmy evening is the perfect antidote to a stuffy day in the office.

The garden at night is a sensual place, where our eyes work differently and our ears and noses are more sensitive than ever. The noises emanating from a wildlife-friendly night garden are incredible: the screech of owls and foxes, the snuffling of hedgehogs and badgers, and the love calls of mating frogs and toads.

'The garden at night is a sensual place, where our eyes work differently and our ears and noses are more sensitive than ever'

Night-flowering plants lure in night-flying insects with their sugary scents. White- and silver-coloured plants reflect moonlight and start to shine after dusk, while stems and branches darken into striking silhouettes, casting sculptural shadows across lawns and up walls.

Nocturnal species of moths are often attracted by sweet smells and pale-coloured plants, using both to navigate by. Jasmine's fragrance is at its most potent at night, which is why it's harvested in the early hours when grown commercially. Tobacco plant also gives off a strong night perfume and its elegant trumpet-shaped flowers are loved by moths. Species like night-scented stock, honeysuckle, mint, evening primrose and soapwort are also good additions to any night garden. »

A pond will draw in night-flying insects, which in turn may attract bats. Bat numbers are in decline due to pesticide use and other environmental pressures decimating their food supplies, so an invertebrate-rich garden can become an important feeding ground.

A pond will, of course, also be loved by frogs and toads. Gardeners should welcome them as they devour that much maligned creature of the night, the slug. Creating a wildlife-friendly pond will provide a home for both of these increasingly threatened amphibians, whose numbers have dropped due to habitat loss. In springtime, the pond at night can pulse with their mating calls.

How to make a hanging night garden

1. Fill a large hanging basket with organic peat-free compost.
2. Plant it with silvery-leaved lavender and strong-smelling sweet rocket, which is also known as 'mother of the evening'.
3. Stand back and admire a tiny hanging night garden that smells and looks gorgeous by the light of the moon.

32.
WATCH ORCHIDS BLOOM
Sedgefield, County Durham

Considered one of the country's most important disused quarry habitats for wildlife, Bishop Middleham Quarry is renowned for the many different species of orchid that can be seen in bloom there.

What will you see?

The reserve was a magnesian limestone quarry which was abandoned in the 1930s and has since been recolonised by a variety of flora representative of magnesian limestone grassland. This is an internationally rare habitat type and is particularly rich in orchid species, such as the pyramidal, common spotted, fragrant, bee, twayblade and, most ▶▶

The rare dark-red
helleborine orchid

> *'Bishop Middleham Quarry is renowned for the many different species of orchid which can be seen in bloom'*

importantly, dark-red helleborine orchid, which, though nationally scarce, can be found in abundance on the reserve. Visit in mid-July to see the orchids in full bloom.

Among the many other plants that flourish on the thin limestone soils are blue moor grass, moonwort, autumn gentian and fairy flax. Extensive areas of common rock rose in the quarry support one of the county's largest colonies of northern brown argus butterflies, which can be seen on the wing in June and July.

The scrub and woodland habitats present on site attract birds from the surrounding farmland and, in 2002, the reserve became only the second recorded breeding site for bee-eaters in the UK, when a pair nested in one of the quarry faces and fledged three young.

Things you should know

- The quarry is home to many butterflies, including certain struggling species, such as the northern brown argus and dingy skipper.
- Visitors should keep to the footpaths as there are several steep cliff faces.
- There are steps all the way down to the quarry floor.
- Dogs must be kept on a lead during spring and summer.

RESERVE NAME: Bishop Middleham Quarry
GRID REF: NZ331326
NEAREST TOWN: Coxhoe or Sedgefield
WILDLIFE TRUST: Durham Wildlife Trust
WEBSITE: www.durhamwt.co.uk
CONTACT: 0191 5843112 / mail@durhamwt.co.uk
TRANSPORT: Limited parking available in laybys near site.
No parking on site; regular bus services from Durham and
Darlington to Coxhoe and Sedgefield

33.
WALK A STONE-AGE MARATHON

Salisbury Plain, Wiltshire

This 26-mile sponsored walk runs between the two World Heritage Sites of Avebury and Stonehenge and is Wiltshire Wildlife Trust's most important annual fundraiser. It takes place on the first Sunday in May every year and around 2,000 people take part, raising money to help protect Wiltshire's wildlife and environment. Shorter walks and a half marathon are also available, as well as parallel events for cyclists and runners with dogs.

What will you see?

The route offers some of the most spectacular scenery across Wiltshire's undulating landscape, not to mention a chance to walk on parts of Salisbury Plain that are normally closed to the public because they're owned by the Ministry of Defence.

Wildlife enthusiasts will delight in seeing skylarks, kestrels, yellowhammers and lapwings flying overhead, while some of the county's most beautifully coloured butterflies, like the green hairstreak, dingy skipper, Duke of Burgundy, marsh fritillary and the common and Adonis blue, are often spotted fluttering about on the plain. For plant aficionados, the chalk downlands offer a springtime visual feast, with orchids, cowslips, milkwort, scabious and knapweed bobbing in the breeze.

The route itself, which takes 8–9 hours, is of historical interest as it traces the approximate trail along which the Sarsen stones were dragged to build Stonehenge in Neolithic times (hence the name of the event). The course is dotted with a number of other significant historical structures, such as Silbury Hill – Neolithic Europe's tallest man-made structure – the Wansdyke – an ancient defence built to fend off the Saxons – and two iron-age hill forts, Rybury Camp and Casterley Camp.

To find out more, visit the Wiltshire Wildlife Trust website at www.wiltshirewildlife.org.

Old Man of Hoy,
Orkney Islands

34.
ISLAND HOP

Who needs the mainland? The British Isles are made up of over a thousand islands full of natural treasures. You could head out to the UK's most northerly reaches, visiting the often mist-wrapped and always beautiful isles of the inner and outer Hebrides, the Orkneys and Shetlands. Visit the Isle of Man or Anglesey in the Irish Sea, or pay tiny Skomer and Skokholm in west Wales a visit.

Down in the most southern parts of Britain you could pop over to the Isles of Scilly archipelago or Alderney far out in the English Channel. Poole Harbour is home to Brownsea Island and other lovely, tiny isles, while the Isle of Wight sits at the very bottom of Britain. Out east, Mersea Island sits in the Thames Estuary and the Isle of Sheppey can be found nestled off the north Kent coast.

Island nature reserves

- Arreton Down and Ningwood Common, Isle of Wight
- Ayres and Scarlett reserves, Isle of Man
- Brownsea Island reserve, Dorset
- Cemlyn and Mariandyrys reserves, Anglesey
- Isle of Muck, Ulster
- Longis and Vau du Saou reserves, Alderney
- Handa Island, Scotland

35.
MAKE ELDERFLOWER CORDIAL

Part of the honeysuckle family, the deciduous elder shrub produces both delicious fruit and delicious flowers. It grows in a rather twisting way with arching branches, reaching a height of about 10 metres. It has greyish-green bark and rather unpleasant-smelling foliage.

The autumn berries start off red before ripening to black, and can be used to make wine and pies. They're a favourite of birds, so make sure you share. Tiny white elderflowers appear in clusters before the fruit in spring, usually blossoming from May until June. They have a sweet, delicate flavour. Pick some and turn them into a cordial that will make long cool summer drinks taste extra special. Elderflower cordial is particularly good with prosecco if you feel like bubbles.

You will need a couple of hours and ...

- 1.5 litres of hot water
- 1 kg of white granulated sugar
- 20 large elderflower heads
- 4 lemons
- 55 g of citric acid

How to do it

1. Locate an elder that's blooming and collect flower heads that are fully open. The flowers lose their freshness quickly so make the cordial as soon after picking as possible.
2. Stir the sugar into the hot water so it dissolves to make a syrup.
3. Grate the lemon zest into a large bowl, then chop the lemons into quarters and pop them in the bowl too.
4. Don't wash your elderflowers but do inspect them for bugs before adding them to the lemons. Once the sugar is fully dissolved, ladle the hot syrup into the bowl and over the lemon and flowers.
5. Stir in the citric acid and cover with a tea towel, then leave to steep overnight, or longer if you can.
6. Strain the mixture through muslin and bottle with tight stoppers.
7. Make sure you seal your potion in a suitably pretty bottle. It will keep for up to a month, but lasts much longer if you freeze it.

36.
VISIT THE ISLES OF SCILLY

Hugh Town, St Mary's

A wondrous archipelago 28 miles off the Cornish coast, the Isles of Scilly are a delight for wildlife lovers and walkers, who can roam the paths that lace the islands.

What will you see?

There is much to see all year round on Scilly. In spring, wildflowers fill the islands with colour and you can get close to friendly blackbirds, wrens and thrushes. At the end of the summer the heathland is bright with yellow gorse and purple heather. Grazing cattle and ponies are used to restore heathland and create habitat for insects, but do mind your step as big oil beetles wander the footpaths. On the coast seabirds abound and you could see razorbill, fulmar, gannets and guillemots, not to mention seals and lots of other marine wildlife.

Scilly is the first landfall from America and many birds, moths and butterflies turn up during the autumn. On a windy day, take a 'Scillonian walk' to see the waves crashing on the rocks or examine the strandline for treasures like cuttlefish bones, crab carapaces and a myriad of shells.

On St Mary's, the largest of the inhabited islands, the Higher Moors Nature Trail goes through wet meadow and reedbeds, with clumps of tussock sedge, giant ferns and small copses of willow. There are two bird hides looking over Porth Hellick Pool, but also look out for eels and young fish feeding at the pool's edge. The path comes to a bank, with views of the sea and beach, where you can bird watch, examine rock pools and look for shells.

From the beach the path goes through pine trees and out on to Salakee Down, a headland of waved heath with spectacular granite tors, where you can explore bronze-age burial chambers and entrance graves. At Giant's Castle find a sheltered spot for sea watching. You may see seals and feeding gannets. If you're lucky you might see a whale! From here, you can carry on along the path that crosses the end of the airport runway to Old Town.

Things you should know

- The Isles of Scilly Wildlife Trust manages 60% of the land mass of Scilly, so you are never far from wildlife wherever you go, including land on the islands of St Agnes, Bryher, Samson and St Martin's, plus a plethora of uninhabited islands.
- Higher Moors Nature Trail has easy access to Porth Hellick. The path to Giant's Castle has inclines in places and temporary stiles when the Trust's conservation cattle are grazing.
- There are regular boat trips to see seals and seabirds, sometimes landing on uninhabited islands which are wildlife sanctuaries.
- You can get there by boat, helicopter or plane.

RESERVE NAME: Isles of Scilly
GRID REF: SV921111
NEAREST TOWN: Hugh Town, St Mary's
WILDLIFE TRUST: Isles of Scilly Wildlife Trust
WEBSITE: www.ios-wildlifetrust.org.uk
CONTACT: 01720 422988 / enquiries@ios-wildlifetrust.org.uk
TRANSPORT: For travel and accommodation info, visit www.simplyscilly.co.uk

37.
VISIT LONGIS RESERVE
Alderney, Channel Islands

Alderney is a tiny island, just 3.5 x 1.5 miles in size, but it's home to two nature reserves run by Alderney Wildlife Trust, as well many other not-to-be-missed wildlife sites. It's possible to see much in one day (though the longer you stay the better, of course!) and arguably nowhere else in the UK can boast so much varied and dramatic scenery in such a small space.

What will you see?

Longis Reserve is at the eastern end of Alderney and is at its best in spring and summer, although in autumn the bird migrations can be spectacular, while in winter wildfowl often throng the reserve's pools and waders appear in impressive numbers along the shoreline. Inland the reserve is mostly calcareous grassland, grazed by the Trust's small herd of Guernsey cattle to encourage the diversity of low-growing plants such as small hare's-ear and wild thyme. The whole area is criss-crossed by a network of paths to allow easy access for walkers. It will take you about one and a half hours to walk a full circuit of the Longis Reserve, but you'll need considerably longer if you're to spend time at the many vantage points and in the bird hides.

There are two ponds in the reserve, each with a hide equipped with binoculars, wall charts and plenty of seating. Longis Pond is a semi-natural water-table pool, set in grassland and almost surrounded

RESERVE NAME: Longis Reserve
GRID REF: 594079
NEAREST TOWN: St Anne
WILDLIFE TRUST: Alderney Wildlife Trust
WEBSITE: www.alderneywildlife.org
CONTACT: 01481 822935 / info@alderneywildlife.org
TRANSPORT: Direct flights from Southampton or indirect via Guernsey; on the island there's a train (weekends in spring and summer only), plus car and bike hire

Mannez Pond

'Arguably nowhere else in the British Isles can boast so much varied and dramatic scenery in such a small space'

by reed beds. It's a good place to see secretive birds, like water rails. Mannez Pond (above) is much larger, lying in an old quarry near the lighthouse, and is a haven for wildfowl in all seasons. Not only is the hide a fine place to watch birds, it's also a great place to observe Alderney's large numbers of dragonflies.

A footpath runs along the spectacular coastline from the lighthouse, past the picturesque Fort Houmet Herbe to Longis Bay. It's mainly level walking, although not suitable for wheelchairs. Interesting flowers grow along this route, like golden samphire, sand crocuses, bastard toadflax, green-winged orchids and the endemic Alderney sea lavender. The area is home to lots of butterflies, including the iconic Glanville fritillary, and day-flying moths, such as the emperor and oak eggar, and the rare pale shoulder moth.

From this part of the island there's a panoramic view of the French coast, only eight miles away, and it's a great place to see Alderney's two tidal races converging, with some of the fiercest seas in the British Isles.

38.
VISIT SKOMER ISLAND

Haverfordwest, Pembrokeshire, Wales

Skomer Island is a National Nature Reserve located off the Pembrokeshire Coast National Park and is the most important seabird site in
southern Britain, with an estimated half a million birds. The island
is owned by the Countryside Council for Wales and managed by the
Wildlife Trust of South and West Wales. In addition to its spectacular
wildlife and scenery, the island is of great archaeological interest and
considerable evidence of prehistoric human occupation can be found
in the form of various huts and enclosures.

What will you see?

The island is open to the public between early spring and late autumn
and provides visitors with a wealth of opportunities to get up close
to wildlife. During May and June the island is carpeted with bluebells
and red campion, with thrift and sea campion seen along cliff edges
later in the year. During this time, seabird colonies, such as puffin,
razorbill, guillemot and kittiwake, can be seen and heard throughout

> *'In addition to its spectacular wildlife and scenery, Skomer Island is of great archaeological interest'*

the island. Skomer also boasts the largest Manx shearwater colony in the world. These birds breed in burrows on the island between April and September.

Although Skomer provides wildlife experiences throughout the year, autumn sees the island at its wildest and yet most tranquil. Visit at this time to witness the spectacular sight of grey seals hauled out on rocks in the numerous coves and beaches to give birth. 2009 saw over 140 newborn seal pups on Skomer. While admiring the newborn seals, look out to sea for common dolphins and harbour porpoises. Wander the island alone at dusk and see the last of the Manx shearwater young making their journey out into the Atlantic Ocean. Amazingly, some will return after several years at sea, often landing near the burrow they were born in.

Things you should know

- Overnight accommodation and volunteering opportunities on the island are available.
- Due to its rugged terrain, the island is not suitable for disabled access. There are gentle walking routes on the reserve but a steep flight of steps from the landing stage.

RESERVE NAME: Skomer Island
GRID REF: SM725095
NEAREST TOWN: Haverfordwest
WILDLIFE TRUST: The Wildlife Trust of South and West Wales
WEBSITE: www.welshwildlife.org
CONTACT: 01239 621212 / info@welshwildlife.org
TRANSPORT: Access to the island is by the Dale Princess ferry from Martin's Haven during the spring–autumn period (Tuesday–Sunday). Car parking, boat and landing fees apply

SUMMER

Summer in the UK is lazy, though never quite long enough. When the weather is perfect, the sun hot and the breeze gentle, there is nothing quite like eating alfresco – taking a picnic to your favourite park, beach or mountain – or finding a private wilderness and indulging in some wild swimming or camping. Warm evenings are perfect for watching after-hours wildlife hunting for food, while choosing to holiday in the UK means a chance to discover and explore fascinating and spectacular new landscapes.

The summer solstice is the longest day of the year and so for many 21 June means that summer has arrived. It's from this point on that we can look forward to some of our best weather, but also some of our most extreme. Torrential rain and raging thunderstorms can leave areas flooded, while exhausting heatwaves can result in water shortages and droughts.

Summer has a soundtrack of humming bees and insects, with grasshoppers and crickets providing some of the most potent sounds of the season. Butterflies are a favourite summer insect, exotic winged

creatures that fill warm air with colour. Small tortoiseshells, red admirals, peacocks, painted ladies, commas, speckled woods, large whites, green-veined whites and small whites might all be spotted in a garden, while a visit to a wildflower-rich grassland or woodland site could reveal rarer species. This is also the season to spot hunting spiders, shield bugs and longhorn beetles.

Many of these insects are after nectar and summer is all about flowers, of course. From June to August look out for whole fields full of bright red poppies, or scatterings of them dotted along road verges, field edges and in towns and cities where building work has disturbed the soil. Head to a heath or moorland site in August and witness a late-summer spectacle: the landscape turning purple with flowering heather. You'll also find the yellow flowers of spiny gorse – on hot summer days the flowers smell like coconut and you can hear the gorse seed heads popping.

Summer is also a great time to watch out for young birds. Fledglings often look different from their parents – for example, young robins are brown with speckled breasts. Look on a local lake or river for ducklings, goslings and cygnets. These young birds have to find their own food but their parents stay close and will keep them warm in cold or wet weather. You may even see young cygnets taking a rest by having a ride on their parent's back. Great crested grebes also carry their young in this way. »

Puffin

*'Warm evenings are perfect for watching
after-hours wildlife hunting for food'*

Summer would simply not be complete without a visit to the coast.
Take a cliff-top walk, watch seabirds breeding, spot seals bobbing and
giant sharks basking, investigate some rock pools, build a sandcastle,
sunbathe and then have a good paddle in the shallows to cool off.
Beach combing is one of the most peaceful ways to while away a few
hours, collecting shells and driftwood as your mind wanders to the
sound of the lapping sea.

Things to do in summer

- Go wild swimming
- Moth watch
- Go rock pooling
- Go pond dipping
- Go wild camping

- See puffins
- Hunt for glow worms
- Go on a bat walk
- Watch nocturnal
  wildlife

39.
SEE PUFFINS

Pint-sized and clown-like, the puffin is one of Britain's best-loved birds and possibly its most exotic-looking, with its striking eye make-up and brightly painted beak. Scotland in summer is the place to see puffins, but there are also important breeding colonies further south in Yorkshire, the Isles of Scilly, Alderney, Skomer and Skokholm. Visit between June and mid July if you want to see them in large numbers.

The puffin is an auk. Its short wings allow it to fly underwater in pursuit of fish. Large wings would be a disadvantage in this respect but small wings do make flying in air rather more difficult, and puffins must beat their wings rapidly to stay aloft. The beak is only distinctively coloured in summer – the large red and grey scutes (or horny plates) together with the fleshy yellow rosette in the corner of the mouth are grown in late winter ready for attracting a mate during the breeding season.

Puffins begin nesting in April, gradually building up in numbers as the egg-laying season approaches. They nest underground in burrows, favouring sites close to cliff tops so the parent birds can come in quickly and then escape again to sea, giving predatory gulls less chance to attack. Herring and lesser black-backed gulls will try to steal food from puffins, while the great black-backed gull will actually kill and eat adult puffins.

Female puffins lay a single egg, usually in the early part of May. Newly hatched chicks look like little dark-grey powder puffs, covered in down so long you can barely see their tiny bills, legs and feet. The chick remains in the burrow for about six weeks, feasting on sand eels delivered direct by both parents.

Towards the end of July the chicks leave the nest under the cover of darkness, making their way down to the cliff edge before launching themselves solo into the night. They're long gone by daybreak and will have no more contact with their parents. Young puffins remain at sea for almost two years before joining a colony and looking for a mate and a burrow. Most don't start breeding until they're five years old. Puffin life expectancy is an impressive 25 years.

If puffins float your boat, try a bit of armchair bird watching courtesy of Alderney Wildlife Trust, who have set up a dedicated 'puffincam' on Burhou Island. Go to the Alderney Wildlife Trust website for details.

40.
FOLLOW A
DRAGONFLY TRAIL

Stanstead Abbotts, Hertfordshire

A flooded former gravel pit, Amwell Nature Reserve is now Hertfordshire's top wetland bird-watching sight. It is also home to the Dragonfly Trail, Hertfordshire's best site for dragonflies, which gives visitors access to a wet meadow with lake views and an abundance of dragonflies and damselflies.

What will you see?

The reserve attracts nationally significant numbers of birds all year round, including the rare bittern, and ducks such as gadwall, shoveler and smew. Autumn passage migrants include osprey, marsh harrier and many wading birds, whilst winter is the best time to visit for ducks and geese and the booming call of bitterns.

From May to September, visitors can follow the Dragonfly Trail, where, with luck, you will be able to spot all nineteen species of dragonflies in Hertfordshire, including the hairy dragonfly, red-eyed damselfly, southern hawker, brown hawker, ruddy and the common darter. You will also see the early marsh orchid, pyramidal orchid and the nationally rare marsh dock.

In spring the reserve is excellent for breeding wetland birds with large numbers of sedge and reed warbler, redshank, snipe, both ringed plovers and several duck species. Following extinction in the 1970s, otters were reintroduced to Hertfordshire here at Amwell in 1991, where they have thrived.

Things you should know

- There are three accessible public hides and a viewing area.
- Although the tracks around the reserve are accessible for all, after wet weather wellies are recommended!
- There is a steep bridge which crosses the Lee Navigation, and two other moderately humped bridges in the reserve.

Common Darter

RESERVE NAME: Amwell Nature Reserve
GRID REF: TL376127
NEAREST TOWN: Stanstead Abbotts
WILDLIFE TRUST: Herts & Middlesex Wildlife Trust
WEBSITE: www.hertswildlifetrust.org.uk
CONTACT: 01727 85890/ info@hmwt.org
TRANSPORT: St Margaret's railway station; by car, follow the A10 and the B181
OTHER RESERVES NEARBY: Rye Meads (TL389103), Balls Wood (TL348106) and King's Meads (TL353143)

41.
BUILD A HABITAT WALL

A habitat wall is a palatial mini-beast hotel where insects can shelter and lay their eggs. It can also be a feeding place for insects and small mammals, and provide them with nesting materials. It makes a striking addition to any garden and is very simple to make.

 *How to do it*

1. Find 3–7 old wooden pallets, ideally the same size, and remove protruding nails.
2. Choose a suitable location. The best spots are level, sheltered and either next to a wall, under a tree or in a shady corner. Habitat walls make great screens and can be built to disguise things like compost heaps or bins.
3. Stack the pallets as evenly as possible flat side down. You could secure them together with long screws if the pallets are uneven or your spot is exposed.
4. Collect material to create dark nooks and crannies in the gaps in the pallets. These are the places where insects can shelter or nest. You can use dead seed heads and stalks, small piles of rocks, old wood or wood with holes drilled in it, bundles of twigs, egg cartons or containers stuffed with straw.
5. Fill the gaps in the pallets with your materials. Use the bottom level for larger items, such as pots, bigger pieces of wood or piles of sticks and leaves. Don't worry if you don't have enough material to hand. You can add more over time as the wall develops.
6. Cover the top of the wall with bark – you could source this from a local tree surgeon. It's best not to disturb old pieces of bark as they may already be sheltering insects.
7. Once you've filled the gaps, leave the wall in peace and give wildlife a chance to establish.

 Or...

On a smaller scale, you could make a mini habitat wall using old bird boxes or similar, stacked together and stuffed with natural materials.

Silver Y moth disguised
against a branch

42.
MOTH WATCH

In the past, moth trapping involved killing the insects and pinning them on boards, but this is no longer the case. These days moths are given the respect they deserve, caught briefly in humane traps and then released without harm. Trapping is an important method of identifying and monitoring species and a moth-watching evening can be an enchanting experience. You can buy specialist moth traps, but for the interested amateur there are other, cheaper options too. Wildlife Trusts and butterfly and moth groups organise events where they set up specialist light traps and in this way you can learn an awful lot about the UK's near 2,500 species.

Moths fly throughout the year, but if you fancy doing some DIY moth spotting at home, muggy, moonless nights between April and October are often best. Look on walls and fences near outside lights and check flowers, fallen fruit and ivy. Alternatively, hang a white sheet over a washing line or fence and shine a strong light on to it. A powerful torch or a lamp fitted with an energy-saving light bulb is good. Moths ➤➤

can be caught or photographed as they settle on the sheet. If you need a closer look you can catch the moths using large, clean, clear containers. Put the pot over the moth, lift one side slightly and very gently chivvy it in with the lid. Once the moth is inside, slide the lid on quickly. Moths are extremely fragile, so avoid handling them and release them into the undergrowth as soon as you can. Take pictures of moths you can't identify as there are several websites that you can go to for help.

Moth facts

- Moth numbers have declined alarmingly in the last 30 years. Climate change, pesticide use, habitat loss and even light pollution may all be to blame.
- Moths are drawn to and disorientated by artificial light and often can't escape.
- There are more species of day-flying moths in the UK than butterflies.
- Butterflies often rest with their wings closed up like a book, while moths' resting positions vary greatly.
- Moths are masters of disguise – the angle shades moth has wings that resemble dead leaves, while the buff tip is almost indistinguishable from a broken birch twig.
- Many female moths use pheromones for long-distance seduction. The males' feathery antennae detect these sex-attracting perfumes, sometimes from miles away.

43.
LITTER PICK

Litter lazily dropped anywhere but a bin can have devastating consequences for wildlife. Not only seriously ugly, non-biodegradable waste in the wrong place pollutes land and water and kills animals. There's simply never any excuse to litter, but people often do. Bins overflow and blow over. If you see litter lying around, take a deep breath, put on some protective gloves and pick it up. If local sites are looking messy, an organised litter-pick shares the pain and is actually a great community-building activity. Let's keep Britain tidy, for people and wildlife!

44.
CAST AN ANIMAL FOOTPRINT

You will need ...

- Plaster of Paris
- An old 500g margarine tub for mixing
- A stick or spoon for stirring
- Water
- A strip of card 10 cm wide and long enough to fit around the footprint
- Paper clips

How to do it

1&2.

3.

4.

5.

1. Find an animal footprint and clear away any twigs and leaves from the area around it.
2. Make a circle with the strip of card, join the ends with the paper clip and push it into the ground around the footprint.
3. Into the margarine tub, mix five tablespoons of dry plaster with water and stir until it is like smooth cream.
4. Pour the plaster into the card collar. Wait 5–10 minutes for it to set, then dig it out.
5. Take the cast home to wash, identify and label.

45.
HABITATS: GRASSLAND

Before the influence of humans, grasslands filled with billowing grasses, colourful wildflowers and the hum of insects were only found in natural clearings in woodlands, above the treeline and at the coast. But once people began clearing woodlands for farming, grasslands flourished and were used for grazing livestock and hay production.

There are several different types of grassland, characterised by their soil types. Acid grassland can be found in both upland and lowland areas where fine-leaved grasses like red and sheep's fescues and common bent grow, alongside wild flowers such as sheep's sorrel, heath bedstraw and pretty blue harebells.

Neutral grassland is associated with clays and silty soils. Green-winged orchids dot the grass with purple, while pepper saxifrage and adder's tongue fern also flourish. The unforgettable song of the skylark fills the air and butterflies like common blue, orange tip and meadow brown dance from flower to flower.

Chalk grassland develops on shallow, lime-rich soils that are poor in nutrients. In spring and summer, these special habitats come to life as swathes of wildflowers, such as cowslips, clustered bellflowers, bee orchids and common twayblades attract fluttering butterflies like chalkhill blues, striking Adonis blues and marbled whites. Chalk grassland can be amazingly species-rich and there are records of up to 40 species being recorded per square metre.

Unfortunately, as agriculture has intensified, so the traditional management techniques of ploughing, reseeding, cutting and grazing have declined. Coupled with the increased use of herbicides and fertilisers, our traditional grasslands are now under threat. The Wildlife Trusts are working on a local level to ensure that traditional management techniques are not lost to the mists of time and that our grasslands thrive.

46.
GO ROCK POOLING

It's easy to lose hours practising the art of rock pooling. Armed with an eagle eye, and perhaps a bucket and small fishing net, the keen rock pooler can discover an enormous number of creatures living in the tiniest puddles of water. Any beach with rocks will be full of rock pools once the tide's gone out. These miniature underwater Amazons host blooming and blood-red sea anemones, creative hermit crabs, steadfast limpets and see-through shrimps.

Rock pooling mainly requires patience and peering, letting your eyes slowly travel around the seaweed-fringed twists and turns of the underwater miniature cliffs and caverns. Gently cast your net through the pool and release the contents into a bucket filled with seawater. Try to identify the different species before you return them to the pool where you found them.

Rock pooling is an important way of surveying coastal areas and monitoring the health of marine wildlife populations. Taking part in an organised coastal survey can produce records that aid conservationists' work to protect important marine and coastal habitats.

You might find ...

- Crustaceans, like barnacles and common prawns, edible, hermit, shore, spider and velvet swimming crabs
- Molluscs, like limpets, mussels, periwinkles and dog whelks
- Anemones, like beadlet, strawberry and snakelock anemones
- Starfish, like cushion starfish and brittle stars
- Fish, like pipefish and shanny

47.
SNORKEL

UK waters aren't known for being that warm but if you're feeling brave, in the middle of a hot summer perhaps, snorkelling in the shallows is a great way to look at underwater wildlife. Do it in the sea and freshwater in places that are known to be safe for swimming. It's not just about admiring fish – you'll also see lots of different types of plants plus interesting land formations, rocks and shells. If the water's cloudy, though, you won't be able to see a thing, so choose somewhere where the water's clear.

Good snorkelling sites

- Abercastle, Pembrokeshire
- Coniston Water, Cumbria
- Drawna Rocks, Cornwall
- Farne Islands, Northumberland
- Kimmeridge Bay, Dorset

A little advice

- You can buy snorkels and masks quite cheaply from most sports shops.
- You could practise at a swimming pool first.
- Wear a T-shirt when snorkelling to avoid getting sunburn.
- A wet suit can make chilly waters a lot more bearable.
- If you aren't a confident swimmer, don't go snorkelling.

48.
WITNESS METAMORPHOSIS

Metamorphosis, meaning to 'change in form' or transform, has provided the inspiration for some rather fantastical stories and legends. However this incredible process happens a thousand times in your back garden. Ladybirds, frogs and dragonflies will all happily metamorphose right under your nose, transforming from one thing into something completely different.

The ladybird

Ladybird larvae hatch from clusters of tiny bright yellow eggs. They each have six legs and a long shape. As they grow rapidly, the larvae shed their skin several times. When they are fully grown, they attach themselves to the stem of plants by their tails. The larval skin then splits down the back, exposing the pupae. This is like a protective shell and is often called the chrysalis. The wrapping protects the insects while they undergo the final stages of metamorphosis, eventually emerging as the familiar spotty adult ladybirds we all know.

The common two-spot and seven-spot ladybirds are not endangered but have been facing tough competition recently from the invasive harlequin ladybird.

The frog

Tadpoles hatch from the jelly-like eggs of the adult frog known as frogspawn. The undeveloped tadpoles have gills and a tail, but are very weak. After about a week they gain the ability to swim. In the next four weeks they grow tiny teeth and their gills begin to disappear. Next they start to grow legs, the head becomes more distinct and the body elongates. Their formerly meagre algae diet now includes dead insects and plants. The arms bulge and then pop out, elbows first. After about ten weeks, the tadpole has become a froglet – a small frog with a tail that gradually gets shorter. Within sixteen weeks it will be a fully grown adult frog. At this stage it becomes carniverous, catching any suitably-sized invertebrates with its long, sticky tongue.

A newly emerged dragonfly

Common frogs have been suffering recently due to habitat destruction and fragmentation, as well as disease. Dig a pond in your garden and help these amphibians out. (See page 124 for pond digging advice.)

The dragonfly

Dragonflies begin their lives as nymphs – strange-looking, wingless creatures that live in the murky depths of ponds and marshes. They can remain as nymphs for a few years, sometimes indulging in a spot of cannibalism: a large dragonfly nymph will happily devour a younger, smaller nymph. Once fully grown, and when the weather is clement, the nymph will crawl out of the water and up the stem of a plant, where it will shed its skin and emerge as a young dragonfly. It must wait for its wings to dry out before beginning its hunt for a mate. Females will then lay their eggs in calm water. After a relatively long and muddy period as a nymph, adult dragonflies only live for a few weeks.

There are many species of dragonfly living in the UK and most are quite common. The Norfolk hawker and southern damselfly have full legal protection, however, and are on the UK Biodiversity Action Plan. The southern damselfly is also on the IUCN Red List.

Badger

49.
STAY UP ALL NIGHT

From dusk until dawn, there's a huge amount of wildlife to see and hear after dark, be that foxes scavenging, bats hunting, moths drinking or birds migrating. Pick a clear night in a spot free of light pollution and your night watch could well be lit by a canopy of constellations. If you want some of the best star gazing in the world, head to Galloway Forest Park in Scotland, which was recently unveiled as the first Dark Sky Park in the UK.

Artificial lighting is important for people and nobody would suggest all lights should be extinguished. However, excessive lighting is often both a waste of energy and bad for wildlife. Artificial lighting can disrupt the natural circadian rhythms of many creatures and can also attract wildlife to inhospitable areas. And the thick cloud of light-polluted smog that often gathers over urban areas means city dwellers rarely see the stars. Sadly, less than 10% of people in the UK can now see the Milky Way from where they live.

It's possible to light areas using a lot less energy and causing minimum disruption to creatures of the night. New LED technology can reduce light spill on to rivers and up into tree canopies, and specialist lighting engineers are coming up with alternatives for polluting sodium lamps all the time. Designing the built environment to be more sustainable and more wildlife friendly makes sense.

Badger and owl watching

Badgers

Badgers prefer broad-leaved woodland close to permanent pasture, but will also come into gardens to feed if you're lucky. Most of the time they'll be searching for earthworms, leather jackets and other invertebrate larvae, which are particularly easy to find in lawns and flower beds.

The best way to see badgers in action is to stake them out in the wild. Look for an active sett – big mounds of excavated soil surrounded by well-worn paths, footprints and latrine holes. Find a good viewing position that's downwind of the sett, not too close and disguised by undergrowth. Establish yourself before sunset, then keep still and quiet and keep your fingers crossed. If the badgers become aware of your presence, leave the site. They won't forage if they think a human is watching.

Owls

Do some research and find areas where owls are known to be active. Wear dark clothes and take binoculars, arriving at your viewing point before sunset. You'll find tawny owls in woodland areas and you're most likely to hear them hooting in autumn. Little owls like low-lying land and farms with thick hedgerows and orchards. They like perching on gateposts, especially at dawn and dusk.

Short-eared owls prefer open countryside with rough grassland and are often active hunting during the day and at dusk. Long-eared owls are secretive and elusive birds, favouring dense conifer forest surrounded by open grassland, while barn owls tend to hunt in farmland, meadows, riverbanks and roadside verges.

Other creatures of the night

- Bats
- Deer
- Foxes
- Glow worms
- Hedgehogs
- Moths
- Otters
- Nightjar
- Nightingale

50.
HABITATS: GARDENS

For many of us the sound of bees buzzing amongst the flowers, the sight of tadpoles emerging from jelly-like frogspawn and the smell of freshly cut grass are our first impressions of nature. And more often than not, it's our very own backyard that these memories come from; little havens for wildlife dotted through the deserts of urban sprawl and intensively managed farmland. In fact, the total of size of all the UK's gardens is bigger than all our National Nature Reserves put together!

From tiny backyards and roof terraces to formal gardens and paddocks, all our gardens are important for wildlife as they offer all kinds of different habitats. A garden pond, for example, can be home to frogs and toads, or even rare great crested newts. Trees and shrubs provide good breeding sites for robins and wrens, as well as shelter for voles and prickly hedgehogs. Blue tits, great tits and greenfinches will all visit a bird feeder attached to a window, while peacock and small tortoiseshell butterflies will flutter around flowers in a window box. Larger gardens may even attract species like grass snakes, badgers, owls and woodpeckers.

And gardens are good for people too. They provide a place where we can relax, enjoy the fresh air and nurture our own little patch of nature. But our gardens and allotments are vanishing fast as they are paved over to create parking spaces, and community spaces are consumed by development. For this reason, The Wildlife Trusts are encouraging people to embrace wildlife-friendly gardening, providing a little space for nature on your doorstep.

51.
GO ON A BAT WALK

There are 17 species of bat in the UK. All British bats are relatively small – the pipistrelle is just 5 cm long, with a wing span of 20 cm and a weight of only 4 g. One of the largest and most widespread is the noctule, which can reach a length of 8 cm and is often mistaken for a swift as it flies high soon after sunset. All European bats feed on insects, from tiny gnats to large beetles, and it's estimated that in one night a pipistrelle can eat up to 3,500 insects. During winter there are few active insects, a lack of food that bats cope with by hibernating.

Bats can be found in grassland, farmland and near waterways and ponds – so long as there are sufficient structures to roost in and woodland strips, hedgerow or other landscape features that provide safe commuting routes for bats between roosts and feeding grounds. Some bats have swapped traditional roosting sites for small crevices in buildings, behind weather boarding or between roofing felt and tiles. You're also likely to find them in caves and tunnels.

There are many myths about bats. The saying 'as blind as a bat' is incorrect as bats can see perfectly well, although not in colour. Bats don't get tangled in long hair when flying as they have excellent night vision. They use echo-location to get about, emitting a high-frequency sound that usually can't be heard by people.

Bat numbers are in decline. This is linked to a loss of roost sites, chemical roof treatments that are toxic to bats, pesticide use depleting food sources and a dramatic loss of feeding sites. For these reasons all bats are protected by law under the Wildlife and Countryside Act. It's illegal to harm bats or disturb their roost sites.

If you want to see bats, go for a stroll at dusk around your local park or nature reserve. Also look out for them near trees (particularly brown long-eared bats) or water, or maybe under a street light, picking off the insects attracted to it. Seek out guided bat walks in your area – many Wildlife Trusts organise them.

If you find you rather enjoy bat spotting and want to distinguish between the species, invest in a bat detector. This simple electronic device picks up the high frequency ultrasonic sounds that bats use to navigate and hunt prey and turns them into sounds audible to human ears.

52.
CREATE A HEDGEHOG HIDEAWAY

Hedgehog populations have declined significantly and this once common species is now found on the UK Biodiversity Action Plan (a rescue plan for our most endangered wildlife). Winter starvation is the greatest threat to their survival, with three quarters of the population dying before they are a year old. The loss of permanent pasture to arable farming and the destruction of valuable hedgerows have seriously reduced suitable hedgehog food and shelter. And garden and agricultural pesticides are inflicting untold damage on hedgehogs, whose diet is predominantly made up of so-called pest species. Many also die on roads.

Hedgehogs need our help. Resisting the urge to be over-tidy in your garden will help to make it a friendlier place for wildlife. Simple things like leaf and log piles make great hiding places for small mammals and insects, and also provide them with nesting materials that they can move elsewhere. Anything that mimics the hedgehog's natural habitat of woodland edge and hedgerow bottom will help.

The easiest way to build a hedgehog shelter is to make a lean-to by placing an old board against a wall or fence and covering it in leaves, compost, soil or branches. The gap under the board will provide a relatively dry shelter where a hedgehog can hibernate. You could rake some dry leaves into the gap or provide a little dry straw for nesting too.

If you're feeling more ambitious, try building a wooden box about 35 cm wide x 40 cm long x 30 cm high. Make an entrance tunnel about 35 cm long with an opening at least 15 cm x 15 cm. Waterproof the top and drill drainage holes in the sides and bottom. Don't use wood preservatives. Hide the box under logs and debris. Pop in some dry grass and leaves for bedding.

Don't disturb your shelter between May and September – if there's a mother inside she may abandon her young.

'Leaf and log piles make great hiding places for small mammals and insects'

Hog facts

- The hedgehog's spines are specially adapted hairs and an adult has about 5,000 of them.
- Strong muscles beneath the skin enable the hedgehog to curl up at the hint of danger.
- Hedgehogs are nocturnal and can cover two miles in a night foraging for food.
- They're good climbers and can scramble up fences and low walls.
- Hedgehogs have poor eyesight but an excellent sense of smell and very good hearing.
- Before mating, the male and female circle each other for hours in a kind of courtship dance.

53.
SEE BRITAIN'S LARGEST BUTTERFLY

Hickling, Norfolk

The Broadland landscape is unique and has a range of habitats, from wild expanses of open marshland near the coast, to wooded areas inland. Consequently, an amazing diversity of wildlife can be found there, including nationally rare species, such as the swallowtail butterfly, fen orchid and Norfolk hawker dragonfly.

What will you see?

At Hickling Broad, the largest and wildest of the Norfolk Broads, birds are everywhere, many of them waterbirds, including ducks, geese and waders. Marsh harriers are a familiar sight, as well as numerous species of woodland birds, like woodpeckers, treecreepers and finches. In the spring, listen for the piping calls of redshanks and oystercatchers as they prepare to nest on the marshland. In summer, migrant warblers join the chorus, such as chiffchaffs, blackcaps and willow warblers, while in winter visitors include siskins and redpolls.

'An amazing diversity of wildlife can be found there, including nationally rare species, such as the swallowtail butterfly, fen orchid and Norfolk hawker dragonfly'

The area is also rich in plant life, with over 250 species recorded in the fens alone, and it's home to mammals, such as otters and water voles. Larger mammals, like roe deer, can be spotted grazing the marshland, as can Norfolk Wildlife Trust's own herd of konik ponies.

Britain's largest butterfly, the swallowtail, has a wingspan of up to 9 cm and stunning yellow and black markings. The swallowtail is now limited to the Norfolk Broads, favouring sites with a vigorous growth of milk parsley, where they lay their eggs on the tallest plants. Although a rare British insect, if you visit Hickling Broad in the early morning on a bright summer's day, you should spot one.

Things you should know

- Follow the boardwalk nature trail through the reed beds and hop on a guided wildlife boat trip.
- A two-hour boat trip includes a visit to an exclusive 18-metre tree tower, where the view of the Broadland area is simply stunning. Pre-booking is advised.
- The visitor centre, toilets, boardwalks and one hide are fully accessible by wheelchairs.

ABOVE LEFT Hickling Broad
BELOW RIGHT Swallowtail butterfly

RESERVE NAME: Hickling Broad
GRID REF: TG428222
NEAREST TOWN: Hickling
WILDLIFE TRUST: Norfolk Wildlife Trust
WEBSITE: www.norfolkwildlifetrust.org.uk
CONTACT: 01692 598276 / email via the website
TRANSPORT: parking on site
OTHER RESERVES NEARBY: Upton Broad and Marshes (TG380137) and Cley Marshes (TG054440)

54.
FLY A KITE

Kite flying is an excuse to get thoroughly windswept and to lose your-self watching clouds shape-shift across the sky. Wait for the wind to pick up, then walk to the top of the highest grassy hill you can find. Large open spaces are best, away from trees and pylons. Catch your breath and admire the view.

Unpack your kite and unravel your strings. Lick your finger and test the direction the breeze is blowing in. Wait for what feels like a good gust and then launch your kite into the wind. Feel immense pride as it glides through the air with beauty and grace.

Lift, gravity, thrust and drag are the forces at work when you fly a kite. Lift is an upward force created by wind pressure on the face of the kite, which makes the kite rise and keeps it in the air. Thrust is the power of the wind that creates lift. Gravity is the downward force on the kite, which works against lift. Drag is the air resistance to the kite as it travels forward. To fly, a kite needs to have enough lift and thrust to overcome gravity and drag.

It's easy to make your own kite out of things you might find around the house. You could use a plastic bag, or perhaps the fabric from a broken umbrella, stretched across a frame constructed from light-weight bamboo sticks or dowelling. Tie pretty old ribbons on to a length of string for a tail.

How to make a kite

1. Make a cross with two sticks – the cross stick should be placed about one third of the way along the main stick. Tie the sticks together securely with string.

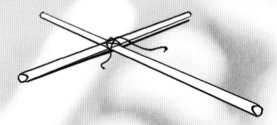

2. Cut a kite shape out of a large plastic bag to fit the frame and tie the ends of the sail to the frame.

3. Tie strings to the cross stick of the frame and attach a tail and some decorations, but be careful not throw things out of balance.

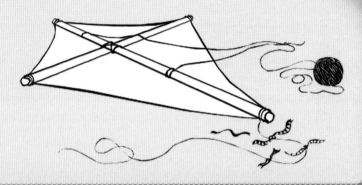

55.
PRESS FLOWERS

Have you ever looked at the profusion of flowers in June and July and wished you could capture some of that summer spirit for the cold winter months?

Pressing flowers is a great way to keep a bit of summertime magic in your life. Shop-bought flower presses are great but pressing flowers doesn't have to involve expensive equipment. You can layer up cardboard and blotting paper in a sandwich to make your own flower press. Layer it cardboard, blotting paper, flower, blotting paper, cardboard and repeat. Your sandwich needs to be weighed down between two heavy books for the best and flattest end results.

Or if you want to keep it really simple, just pop your flowers in between the pages of an old book. An old phone book works well. Come back in a month and your flowers will be ready.

Try to choose flowers which have no fleshy parts. Grasses can create interesting shapes and textures and larger flowers like roses work better pressed as individual petals. Have fun and experiment.

What to do with your pressed flowers:

- Make your own flower design and frame it
- Make home-made greeting cards
- Make your own flowery bookmark

56.
USE BINOCULARS

A pair of "bins" is an incredibly important tool for the naturalist, whether you're an amateur or a pro. A few simple adjustments will set up your binoculars so they are perfect for you. The first thing to do is to make sure you have the right distance between the eye cups. Hold them up to your face and pivot them until you have a nice clear circle of view. You shouldn't see things in two circles, just one. If you wear glasses, make sure the eye caps are fully pushed in; if you don't, make sure they're fully extended.

Next you need to play with your diopta – this is the plus/minus dial found on one of the eye pieces or occasionally on the top of the bins. Cover the outward-facing lens on the diopta side of the binoculars with your palm. Keeping both eyes open and the diopta side covered, hold the bins up to your eyes, then use the main focus wheel to adjust the view you see until it's absolutely crisp. If you focus on something with texture, like a hedge or tree, it makes it easier.

Once that view is sharp, cover up the other lens, again keeping both eyes open. Using the diopta dial this time rather than the main focus wheel, turn it until the view is crystal clear. Now when you look through the bins with both eyes and neither side covered, you should have a perfect view. You could use a bit of paint to mark the spot where your dials need to be, as it's easy for them to get knocked.

'A pair of "bins" is an incredibly important tool, whether you're an amateur or a pro'

57.
EXPLORE A GRAVEYARD

Cemeteries and graveyards are brilliant places to spot wildlife. Quiet and undisturbed, many species seek them out as peaceful refuges where they can find food and shelter. Think of the churchyards in your area as little nature reserves waiting to be discovered.

Graveyards tend to be semi-natural grassland, a species-rich habitat, often with lots of flowers and grasses. In some cases this may take the form of long meadow grasses, dotted with flowering plants like ox-eye daisy, common poppy and yellow rattle, giving the cemetery a hay meadow sort of feel. In other cases the grass may be much shorter, allowing flowers like bird's-foot trefoil or orchids to grow.

Creatures associated with cemeteries and graveyards include wood-land-edge species like bats, spotted flycatchers, tawny owls and song thrushes, as well as foxes and plenty of butterflies. Headstones have ❯❯

an ecology all of their own – lichens love them. Of the 1,700 British species, over 300 have been found growing on churchyard stone in lowland England and many cemeteries play host to well over 100 species. Lichens are sensitive to changes in their environment and scientists can use them to monitor air pollution. Some species are only found where the air is clean, while other species thrive in the nitrogen-rich, dirtier air that's common in cities.

The wealth of species that can be found in graveyards is now being recognised, and many have been designated as Sites of Special Scientific Interest.

58.
MAKE A MINI NATURE RESERVE

Heading off to your favourite nature reserve or discovering a new one is great, but wouldn't it be nice to have one on your doorstep as well? A tiny, low-maintenance one, of course.

You will need ...

- A window box
- A small log
- A yoghurt pot
- A rock
- Some peat-free compost

How to do it

1. Fill the box with compost and then add a few features – dig in the yoghurt pot, fill it with rainwater and add the small log and rock.
2. Choose a safe place to put your window box – somewhere like an old bench or wall at an easy height for inspection.
3. Watch and wait. Keep a diary. Record the changes you see. Look under the rock and log for small creatures.
4. Think about land management. Remove out-of-control plants or cut them back with scissors.

Check out the original windowbox nature reserve
at windowboxwildlife.blogspot.com

59.
USE A SWEEP NET

Sweep nets look a bit like a larger version of the nets you might use to go rockpooling at the seaside. They tend to have a cloth net and are generally used for surveying insects. Try using one in a grassland in the summer and you'll get a real insight into just how much wildlife there is, most of it usually out of sight.

Sweep nets have been used by naturalists for hundreds of years. Hold one in your hand and it's hard not to feel like a Victorian beetle hunter ready to swish through meadows and woodlands across Britain in search of rare insects. These days you can buy sweep nets from a range of online suppliers.

Using one is fairly simple but you need to be careful and make sure you don't damage any wildlife.

What to do

- Hold the net with the hoop end nearest to the ground in front of you.

- Slightly tilt the net back so the bottom edge is the leading edge. This will help to stop things falling out.

- Swing the net from side to side in front of you - a full swing from one side to the other. Try sweeping roughly once per step as you walk through the field.

- In short vegetation, swing the net as deeply as possible. When vegetation is taller, sweep deeply enough to just keep the upper edge of the sweep net above the plants.

- Stop every now and then to examine your findings. Gently hold the net closed with one hand, to stop creatures flying away, while you get ready to have a closer look. Once you've had a look (remember to take a magnifying glass with you), gently release your captives back to where they came from.

60.
GO WILDLIFE WATCHING AT BALLOO WETLAND

Bangor, County Down

Balloo Wetland is a brand-new nature reserve established in partnership with the local council from an old brownfield site. Through the creation of ponds, grasslands, hedges and woodland, the site has been transformed into a haven for wildlife. Tucked away in the heart of an industrial estate, the wetland offers a quiet sanctuary for a broad range of plants and animals. A network of paths, boardwalks and dipping platforms allow easy access for all types of visitors.

What will you see?

The reserve has several distinct habitats, including woodland, scrub, grassland, ponds and reed beds. The grassland area of the reserve supports a wide array of native plants and flowers, such as yellow rattle, tormentil, cuckoo flower, ragged robin, black medick and bird's-foot trefoil. Part of the reserve has been planted up as native woodland,

> *'Tucked away in the heart of an industrial estate, the wetland offers a quiet sanctuary for a broad range of plants and animals'*

with species like blackthorn, hazel, spindle and holly, so this new reserve will continue to change and mature for many years to come. There is also a bird hide which overlooks a magnificent pond, an ideal location to spot waterfowl and waders.

The best time to visit Balloo Wetland is in the spring and summer months when the reserve comes alive with the sound of insects and birds and the meadow shimmers with colour. The reserve hosts African migrant birds, like willow warblers, and the ponds attract swallows, house martins and sand martins. The adjacent gorse scrubland has several interesting species, such as stonechats, whitethroats and reed buntings.

In winter the ponds are visited by mallards, teals and goldeneyes. Buzzards, kestrels, sparrowhawks and the occasional merlin are also a particular treat. Watch out for roving flocks of tits, like the long-tailed tit, and finches, such as redpolls, linnets and goldfinches.

Things you should know

- The reserve has disabled access and is buggy friendly, with over half a mile of boardwalk paths leading around the site.
- There's a picnic area for alfresco feasting.
- Don't forget your binoculars.

RESERVE NAME: Balloo Wetland
GRID REF: IJ792505
NEAREST TOWN: Bangor
WILDLIFE TRUST: Ulster Wildlife Trust
WEBSITE: www.ulsterwildlifetrust.org
CONTACT: 028 4483 0282 / info@ulsterwildlifetrust.org
TRANSPORT: Bangor railway station; parking on site
OTHER RESERVES NEARBY: Balloo Woodland (IJ795508)

61.
HABITATS: HEATHLAND

Familiar as wide, open landscapes peppered with the yellow of gorse and purple of heathers, more than 80% of our lowland heaths have been destroyed since the 19th century. Even rarer than rainforest, heathland is one of our most threatened habitats.

For thousands of years, heathlands were used by local people for grazing livestock and gathering materials. Gorse was used for fires, bracken for animal bedding, sand and gravel for building, and bilberries and fungi for food. These traditions have slowly been lost to the march of civilisation and our heathlands have been built upon, turned into farmland or planted with non-native conifers.

Those that are left, however, support a whole host of wildlife. Bees buzz around the bulbous blooms of bell heather and more delicate stems of ling heather. Adders and common lizards bask in the sun on bare patches of ground, while metallic green tiger beetles scuttle across sandy soils. In wetter areas, sphagnum mosses form a spongy, sopping layer and sundews glisten in the sun, waiting to ensnare unsuspecting flies.

The scattered cover provides ideal conditions for breeding birds. Listen out for the distinctive 'churring' of a male nightjar on a balmy summer evening; superbly camouflaged by their grey-brown mottled plumage, they nest on the ground. Much more conspicuous is the Dartford warbler, often spotted perched on a prominent gorse branch singing its heart out.

The Wildlife Trusts are working to restore and protect our heaths by clearing encroaching scrub, campaigning for protection from development and encouraging local people not to disturb ground-nesting birds. This work is vital if our rare heathland wildlife is to survive.

PICTURED Coastal heathland

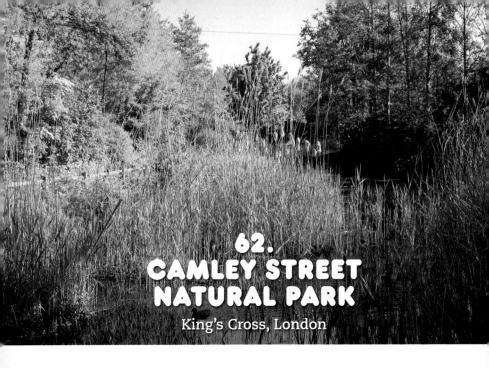

62.
CAMLEY STREET NATURAL PARK

King's Cross, London

Eight thousand unique square metres of wild green space right in the heart of London, this innovative and internationally acclaimed nature reserve on the banks of the Regent's Canal is a place for both people and wildlife.

What will you see?

Camley Street Natural Park was created from an old coal yard back in 1984. It sits just north of St Pancras and King's Cross stations and is popular with all kinds of people seeking respite from the buzz

RESERVE NAME: Camley Street Natural Park
GRID REF: TQ299834
NEAREST TOWN: London
WILDLIFE TRUST: London Wildlife Trust
WEBSITE: www.wildlondon.org.uk
CONTACT: 020 7833 2311 / camleyst@wildlondon.org.uk
TRANSPORT: King's Cross St Pancras station; numerous buses; no parking
OTHER RESERVES NEARBY: East Reservoir Community Garden (TQ323871) and Centre for Wildlife Gardening (TQ338755)

'Camley Street is popular with all kinds of people seeking respite from the buzz of the city around them'

of the city around them, as well as being a hub for London Wildlife Trust volunteers.

The reserve has a visitor centre and provides natural habitat for birds, butterflies, amphibians and a rich variety of plant life. Special features include pond, meadow and woodland, and species you might spot include rare earthstar fungi, reed warblers, kingfishers, geese, mallards, herons, reed buntings and bats.

Things you should know

- Join a guided bat or moth walk in late summer, or indulge in a spot of pond dipping.
- The reserve is always looking for volunteers to help out, especially during their busier times. Please check their website for more details.
- The reserve is open from 10am until 5pm, seven days a week.

63.
MAKE LAND ART

Land art, or earth art, refers to a branch of the conceptual art movement that emerged in the 1960s and 1970s. Land artists work in and with the landscape, often using photography and maps to document pieces sculpted directly into or on to the earth, or structures constructed from found natural materials like rock and wood.

The works frequently exist in the open, located well away from civilisation, and are left to change and erode through exposure to the elements. Land art is also exhibited in galleries in the shape of installations created from natural materials. Well-known land artists include Robert Smithson, Andy Goldsworthy, Richard Long, Walter de Maria, Michael Heizer and Denis Oppenheim.

Land art is all about scale and celebrating the immense beauty of natural landscapes. Take inspiration from the great earth workers and create some land art of your own. Place some stones in an interesting pattern or plot out a walk with a route that forms an aesthetically pleasing shape on a map. Or write about your experiences. Richard Long's work often describes epic walks he has undertaken and can be text rather than picture-based.

64.
GO WILD SWIMMING

Wild swimming is about swimming in places other than swimming pools. It's about leaving overheated, chlorinated water behind and bathing in streams, rivers, lakes, lagoons, lochs and seas. It can mean ambitious and athletic journeys across wide stretches of wild water or it can mean gently floating in sun-warmed shallows, with pond weed between your toes and ducks bobbing by your head.

It can be something solitary or something shared. It can be a riot and it can be romantic. It was the late, great naturalist Roger Deakin who coined the phrase 'wild swimming', when he wrote about his deep love of an age-old outdoor pursuit, which allowed him to get incredibly close to wildlife.

'Wild swimming can be something solitary or something shared. A riot or romantic'

A few considerations

- If you're wild swimming, just as when you walk, cycle or picnic, always respect people and wildlife that live in the area. Leave the area exactly as it was before you arrived. Never pollute it. If a landowner asks you to leave, do so politely.

- In England and Wales there's actually no automatic right to swim in many wild waters, although the Countryside and Rights Of Way Act has opened up more of the countryside. It's different in Scotland, where you can access all inland waters if you stick to the Outdoor Access Code. Get the most out of the your wild swimming trip by doing your research and checking that your chosen location is safe and suitable.

- Britain's wild waters can be very cold so, if you're just starting out, pick a hot summer's day and remember to take warm clothes to wrap up in post swim. Keep active – a good way to wild swim is to combine it with a long wild walk.

65.
GO RIVER-DIPPING

Bourton-on-the-Water, Gloucestershire

Greystones Farm Nature Reserve is tucked away on the outskirts of Bourton-on–the-Water in the Cotswolds and is a short walk from the town centre. The meadows are one of the richest and largest examples of this habitat in the Cotswolds, and are home to uncommon plants such as southern marsh orchids and early marsh orchids.

What will you see?

The beautiful meandering River Eye runs through Greystones Farm Nature Reserve and the River Dickler borders the site. If you followed these rivers you would end up in London, as they're tributaries of the River Thames. On a sunny day, the riverbanks provide perfect picnic spots – maybe even dip your toes in and feel the fish tickle them as they swim by. Take nets and wellies to while away hours dipping in the river and discovering what wildlife you can catch. Play poohsticks from the bridges.

Eagle-eyed visitors looking at the mud on the riverbanks may spot the footprints and tracks of the elusive otter and the threatened

'These meadows are one of the richest and largest examples of this habitat in the Cotswolds'

water vole, which Gloucestershire Wildlife Trust is campaigning to save from extinction in the Cotswolds.

Take the opportunity to lie in the middle of a meadow and watch the clouds as they pass by and listen to nature – the sounds of buzzing bees as they visit the wildflowers.

RESERVE NAME: Greystones Farm Nature Reserve
GRID REF: SP173209
NEAREST TOWN: Bourton-on-the-Water
WILDLIFE TRUST: Gloucestershire Wildlife Trust
WEBSITE: www.gloucestershirewildlifetrust.co.uk
CONTACT: 01451 810853
TRANSPORT: Pay-and-display parking 300 m from site; take the A429 north until you reach Bourton-on-the-Water
OTHER RESERVES NEARBY: Whelford Pools in the Cotswold Water Park

66.
DISCOVER TOLKIEN'S INSPIRATION

Birmingham, West Midlands

Moseley Bog and Joy's Wood Local Nature Reserve is a green oasis where the sounds of the city seem to disappear and are replaced by birdsong and the hum of insects. It has a unique character: damp woodland surrounded by ancient trees and with a mysterious bog at its heart. So journey into its green depths, close your eyes and imagine – but don't fall asleep leaning against one of the old willows!

What will you see?

Moseley Bog was the childhood haunt of JRR Tolkien, and he would have seen the same array of old trees, birds and colourful wild flowers that can still be seen today. Other nearby Birmingham landmarks are thought to have inspired places in *The Hobbit* and *The Lord of the Rings*, and Moseley Bog provided the inspiration for the Old Forest. Each May there are Tolkien-themed events, including guided walks and open-air theatre, at Moseley Bog and elsewhere in the Shire Country Park.

In spring look out for a spectacular display of bluebells in the old woodland of Moseley Bog, while in summer, colourful butterflies chase around the newer glades of the adjacent Joy's Wood.

History buffs should look out for the remains of a former mill dam and an ancient monument comprising two Bronze-Age burnt mounds.

RESERVE NAME: Moseley Bog and Joy's Wood Local Nature Reserve
GRID REF: SP093820
NEAREST TOWN: Moseley, Birmingham
WILDLIFE TRUST: The Wildlife Trust for Birmingham and the Black Country
WEBSITE: www.bbcwildlife.org.uk
CONTACT: 0121 454 1199 / info@bbcwildlife.org.uk
OTHER RESERVES NEARBY: Sarehole Mill, the inspiration for Hobbiton Mill (SP099818)

67.
GO WILD CAMPING

Forget luxury yurts and all-singing, all-dancing motor homes: wild camping is the ultimate in minimalistic travel. It's about leaving the madding crowd far behind and eschewing hot showers and flushing loos. To get the most out of a wild camping trip you need to be well prepared and aware of laws around camping and access to the countryside, so it's worth doing your research before you set off.

Plan your trip, study some maps and make sure you know about the area you are heading for. Choose a time when the weather is fine and the evenings long. Pack a lightweight tent, sleeping bag and bare essentials in a backpack and set out. Find a suitable spot, pitch up and watch night roll in. Breakfast in the dew, pack up and move on.

'Waking up as dawn cracks over a deserted landscape is a glorious experience'

Leaving the romance of it all behind, there are a few things to consider before you camp wild. In England and Wales there's no legal right to do it and permission should be sought from landowners. This is not always practical and in mountainous areas and hill land, wild camping is generally accepted as long as it's for a limited time, is discreet – out of sight of houses and farms – and is low impact. If the landowner asks you to move on you should, but seasoned wild campers say they rarely are.

Wild camping is about respecting your environment. The Forestry Commission and National Trust are clear that they don't allow wild camping on their land. Nature reserves are not good places for wild camping as they are often environmentally very sensitive and protect endangered wildlife. Some National Parks welcome wild camping, as long as you

Essential packing

- A tent
- A map
- Insect repellent
- Warm and waterproof clothes
- A blanket or sleeping bag
- Drinking water

»

act responsibly but you should still get permission from landowners. Helpfully, the Dartmoor National Park Authority have a map of areas of common ground for wild camping and in Wales the Brecon Beacons National Park provides a list of farms that welcome wild campers. The law is different in Scotland, where wild camping is completely legal and well accepted.

The wild camping code

- Only light fires if you have permission.
- Remember people make a living from the land.
- Respect wildlife.
- Keep quiet and be discreet.
- Wipe away all traces of your stay. Leave the land exactly as you found it.

68.
SIT AND DO NOTHING

What could be wilder than sitting or lying down and immersing yourself in nature by doing nothing for as long as possible. Drink in the smells, sights and sounds. If you stay in one place long enough, are quiet and look closely, chances are, you'll start to see more wildlife too, as encouraged by the lack of human activity creatures lose their inhibitions.

You could lie in long meadow grass looking up at nodding flower heads and grasses with butterflies and bees buzzing above you. Sit in the heather on a dry and dusty heathland and wait for reptiles. Sit in a woodland clearing and wait for birds to reveal themselves. Or just spend half an hour in the corner of your garden observing the comings and goings in your flowerbeds from ground level.

69.
GLOW-WORM SPOTTING
Bedfordshire, Cambridgeshire and Northamptonshire

Glow worms can be spotted across Britain but are more common towards the south. They are said to favour chalky or limestone areas, so grassland nature reserves are a good place to begin your quest. Try the Wildlife Trust nature reserves at Old Sulehay in Northamptonshire, Totternhoe in Bedfordshire and Cherry Hinton Chalk Pits and Brampton Wood in Cambridgeshire. Visit the Trust website for details: www.wildlifebcnp.org.

What will you see?

The best time to look for glow worms is during July. They start glowing as soon as it gets dark and will glow for a few hours, so dusk is a good time to seek them out. It's probably a good idea to take a torch with you so that you can find your footing in the dark, but turn it off when you begin your hunt – the darker it is the easier it will be to spot the glow, which looks like a small green LED light. They like to eat small snails, so if you see these you might get lucky and spot some glow worms too.

Glow-worm facts

- Only the wingless adult female glows in a bid to attract flying males. Once she has mated her light goes out. She lays her eggs and then she dies.
- Adult glow worms can't feed, so they only live for around 14 days.
- Despite the name, the glow worm is not a worm but a small beetle.
- The light they emit is a form of bioluminescence. It's caused when a molecule called luciferin is oxidised to produce oxyluciferin.

70.
GO POND DIPPING

Pond dipping is a fun family activity but be careful and never allow your children to go near water unsupervised.

You will need ...

- A pond or stream to dip in
- Wellingtons and waterproofs
- A net, shallow tray or bowl
- A magnifying glass and a field guide
- A notebook and camera

How to do it

1. Locate a suitable pond to go dipping in.
2. Put a small amount of pond water into your tray/bowl.
3. Dip your net in the pond and pull it through the water – try making a figure of eight.
4. Empty your net into the tray/bowl and examine what you find using your magnifying glass.
5. Use a camera, sketchbook and notes to record the results of your dipping. Field guides are useful for identification.
6. When you've finished, gently empty the water and creatures back into the pond. Disinfect your net when you get home.

71.
VISIT FLAMBOROUGH CLIFFS
Bridlington, Yorkshire

Flamborough Cliffs Nature Reserve is part of the Flamborough Headland Heritage Coast. The site is internationally important for marine wildlife and seabirds. Large numbers nest here in the spring and summer, with fantastic views of puffins, razorbills, guillemots, kittiwakes and fulmars from the cliff-top path.

What will you see?

Erosion by the sea has formed impressive bays, stacks, arches and caves in the chalk cliffs. The reserve provides many unique habitats, which include sea caves – home to specialised algae and rare lichens – and cliff top grassland that supports many plants. Some are typical chalk grassland species, such as kidney vetch, salad burnet and pyramidal orchid; others are maritime specialties, such as thrift and sea plantain. Wet flushes on the slopes also support northern marsh orchid and marsh marigold.

Linnets and yellowhammers use the hedgerows for breeding, occasionally joined by corn buntings. Flamborough is also an important feeding and sheltering point for migratory birds in spring and autumn. Fieldfares and redwings can be seen in their hundreds.

In the summer small tortoiseshell, meadow brown and painted lady butterflies, as well as several species of bumblebee, may be found in sheltered areas. Mammals regularly seen at Flamborough include bank voles, stoats, weasels and foxes.

You should know

- The 45-minute summer boat trip from North Landing showcases the spectacular chalk cliffs of the Flamborough headland, with a commentary from the Trust's marine education team. Booking is essential. Call the Trust to book a Living Seas Safari.

RESERVE NAME:
Flamborough Cliffs
GRID REF: TA240722
NEAREST TOWN:
Bridlington
WILDLIFE TRUST: Yorkshire
Wildlife Trust
WEBSITE: www.ywt.org.uk
CONTACT: 01904 659570 /
info@ywt.org.uk
TRANSPORT: Bridlington
railway station; bus from
Bridlington; parking on site
OTHER RESERVES NEARBY:
Filey Dams (TA107807)

Basking shark

72.
BASK WITH SHARKS

Bask in the summer sun and see if you can catch a glimpse of the UK's largest fish, the basking shark. Organised boat trips with certified operators or a chance sighting on a clifftop stroll are your best bet. During the summer months, Cornish, Devon, Manx, Irish and Scottish waters become regular feeding grounds for basking sharks. Growing up to 12 m long and sometimes weighing as much as 7 tonnes, they feed on plankton, filtering 1,000 to 2,000 m³ of seawater every hour to extract their tiny prey.

The basking shark is an internationally recognised endangered species with legal protection. Its enormous fins are a delicacy in the Far East and are valued highly. Hunting remains the single biggest threat to its future.

Relatively little is known about this giant fish, which makes conservation difficult. Without accurate population numbers it's difficult to tell whether populations are in recovery or decline, and without a clear idea about their most favoured feeding sites, it's hard to know what conservation strategies will be the most effective or which sites need further protection. In response to this need for information, The Wildlife Trusts and other conservation bodies are carrying out much surveying and monitoring work.

Where?

One of the best places in the UK to see basking sharks is around the Lizard Peninsula in Cornwall and also off Land's End. The west coast of Scotland and the Isle of Man are also good places to see basking sharks but sightings are still relatively uncommon so you'll need to keep your eyes peeled.

73.
COLLECT SHELLS

Ever dug your hands deep into your pockets and pulled out a dusty sea shell that's brought happy memories of a day at the beach flooding back? We all become a little magpie-like when we paddle along the shoreline and see pearly objects glinting back up at us.

The desire to collect pretty shells is hard to resist. And UK beaches are fabulous places for finding real beauties. From miniscule to massive, shells positively litter some beaches. Sea-worn pebbles and smooth beads of beaten glass are also great little trinkets, and look great in a jar or creatively strewn. But don't take too many, a handful should be enough.

You might find ...

- Bivalve mollusc
- Chinaman's hat
- Common pelican's foot
- Key hole limpet
- Lagoon cockle
- Needle whelk
- Queen's scallop
- Smooth Venus
- Spiny cockle
- Thin tellin

74.
GO CETACEAN WATCHING

UK seas are home to several species of cetaceans, the group of marine creatures that includes whales, dolphins and porpoises. In British waters you could see minke whales, killer whales and pilot whales, even humpback, fin and sperm whales if you're very lucky. Harbour porpoises, bottlenose dolphins and common dolphins are probably the easiest to spot if you go to the right places.

Cetaceans are highly specialised mammals, living entirely in water but breathing air. They're warm-blooded and give birth to live young, which the mother suckles on milk secreted by mammary glands. Cetaceans are social animals and dolphins in particular have a reputation not only for their sociability with each other, but also with humans.

Cetaceans are divided into two groups. The toothed whales group includes small whales, dolphins and porpoises, all of which prey on fish and squid. The other group is made up of the larger baleen whales. Members of this group feed on microscopic sea life called plankton. They extract plankton from the sea by filtering water through their baleen plates, which are a special upper jaw adaptation.

The harbour porpoise is probably our most common cetacean and also our smallest. They're also known as 'puffing pigs' because of the noises they make when they spout. They live in small groups up to five strong and, unlike their dolphin cousins, they don't leap out of the water in play. Harbour porpoises are quite elusive so you're most likely to see them from a boat.

The common dolphin is a more southern species of dolphin, but recorded sightings appear to be moving further north, possibly due to increasing sea temperatures. Common dolphins are the most numerous dolphins in the world. They're extremely sociable and sometimes whole groups can be seen leaping in the air at one time.

»

Common Dolphin

More playful, bottlenose dolphins are the species that give most people delight. Often found close to shore, they put on displays and will approach boats and even jetskis.

Threats

The health of our dolphins is suffering and numbers are declining because of pollutants we put into the water. Insecticides and PCBs (used in the plastics industry) can upset dolphins, weakening their immune system and impairing their breathing. Entanglement in fishing nets can also be a threat, and this can mean that dolphins and porpoises are caught and die needlessly.

Cornwall Wildlife Trust is working with local fisherman to trial a pinger – a device that can be fitted to fishing nets and which alerts cetaceans to their presence.

Where to see what

- Cardigan Bay, Cardiganshire, for bottlenose dolphins
- The Hebrides and Isles of Scilly for minke whales
- The English Channel for common dolphins
- The North Wales coast for harbour porpoises
- Cornwall for good all-round cetacean watching
- Moray Firth, Scotland, for bottlenose dolphins
- The Isle of Man for good all-round cetacean watching

75.
ROW AND PUNT

There's no better way to spend a summer's day than by heading out onto the river. Give your aching arms a rest, lie back and close your eyes. Feel the sun on your face as you breathe in the smells of the river and listen to the waterbirds gently call to each other. Look out for kingfishers and herons, and listen out for the telltale plop of a water vole. Just keep an eye on your paddles!

76.
PLAY POOHSTICKS

It's easy to keep yourself entertained if you can find some flowing water and a few sticks. Select your stick (make sure you choose a winner), while your opponents do likewise. Each stick should have its own distinct personality, so that you can distinguish your twig from everyone else's. Pick a starting point upriver and agree upon a finishing line downriver. It's more fun if the sticks have to pass under a bridge or over obstacles, like some rocks or a small waterfall.

On the count of three, everyone launches their poohstick into the water. Chase the sticks as they race along. Yell encouragement. Curse loudly when your stick gets stuck. The winner is the owner of the stick that crosses the finish line first. Be prepared to argue if it's a close call and then gloat massively if you emerge victorious. Continue to play as you make your way down the river, until you all fall out.

Poohsticks was first played by that hero of children's literature, Winnie the Pooh, and his friends Christopher Robin, Eeyore and Tigger. Author A.A. Milne originally invented the game to keep his son entertained. Traditionally poohsticks is played by dropping sticks from the upstream side of a bridge and seeing which stick emerges first on the other side.

AUTUMN

Autumn provides a burst of colour and activity after the burned and browning end of summer and before the crisp quietness of winter. The spectrum of brilliant colours that the leaves turn is an eye opener every year. Welly-clad and wading through woodland that is thickly carpeted with crispy leaves, it's hard not to feel young at heart and light of mind. Autumn is the time to hunt for conkers and fungi, bursting up all over the place in weird and wonderful forms, and to preserve foraged fruit in pies and jam.

This is the season when the days are rapidly getting shorter and the sun is becoming lower in the sky. The autumn equinox, when day and night are of equal length, is on 23 September (unless it's a leap year when it falls on the 22nd). There are often spectacular sunsets in autumn. The stars can seem brighter at night, and on some mornings mist hangs luxuriously low over fields and parks. Autumn means wonderful hedgerow harvests of blackberries, rose hips, crab apples, hazelnuts and seeds. Many wildlife species take advantage of this abundance of food to build up reserves of fat for migration or for hibernation.

Autumn is great for watching deer. This is the time of year of the rut – when stags and bucks develop antlers and fight rival males to attract a harem of females. Red deer are our largest land mammal and the stags have the most spectacular antlers of any British species. Deer are widespread and at this time of year you may hear the barking of muntjac and roe deer or the roaring of red deer at night. If you like photography, you can get some great autumnal shots of deer with bracken knotted in their antlers or creating plumes of steam when they breathe out into cool air on crisp mornings.

Many birds form flocks in autumn, from smallish parties of long-tailed tits to huge flocks of waders on coastal estuaries. Look out

The arrival of fieldfares is a sure fire sign autumn is here

for flocks of jackdaws, rooks and carrion crows flying to woodland roosts on autumn evenings. If you live near the coast you could see great skeins of migratory geese arriving from Arctic breeding grounds to overwinter in the UK.

If you have a garden this is a good time of year to clean out any nest boxes that have been used throughout the summer, but only do this when you are absolutely certain they're no longer in use. Remove old nests as this will make sure there is room for a new nest next year and reduce the risk of parasites. Also think about creating log piles and sheltered areas where insects and mammals, like hedgehogs, can hibernate over the winter.

Things to do in autumn

- Play conkers
- Build a pond
- Go blackberrying
- Mulch your garden
- Eat apples
- Make jam
- Walk in the woods
- Hunt for fungi

77.
MAKE A MAP

A map is a diagram showing the arrangement of things. They're a very human way of interpreting the heavens and the earth. Cartography can be traced back to cave paintings and the language of maps could be described as universal. When you visit somewhere regularly, the urge to create a picture of that place can become quite strong. You might want to remember a route, make a note of the location of species you have seen or record how the landscape is changing.

There are several programs online that will help you to create your own maps, plotting out routes and highlighting landmarks. Some also let you share the information with friends online. You could also invest in more advanced software such as a GPS tool that will enable you to locate your position on the Earth.

Or how about handcrafting maps of the lesser-known places in your life as a way of recording the time you have spent there or sharing that spot with someone else? A hand-drawn map of a favourite walk, done carefully on the most beautiful paper you can find, makes a wonderful gift.

Map-drawing tips

- Maps are usually drawn from plan view, so looking down from above.
- Include a north arrow on your map: usually it points towards the top of the page.
- Include a scale – for example, 5 cm = 500 m.
- Use technical pens with nibs of varying thickness, so you can use line weight to distinguish between different types of borders and paths or highlight geographical features.
- Use different-sized fonts to denote the size or importance of named places.
- Mark landmarks on the map using simple but evocative illustrations or symbols.
- Include contours to highlight hilly ground – tightly packed ones will effectively warn people of steep slopes.
- Include a key to decoding your map.
- Always remember to mark an 'x' where the buried treasure is.

78.
FIND FOSSILS

Fancy indulging in a spot of palaeontology? The UK is full of fossils – bits of petrified prehistoric plant and animal imprinted in stone. Study a geological map of the country to see it split into regions ranging from Palaeogene through Jurassic to Cambrian. You could join an organised fossil hunt or go it alone at locations stretching across the UK.

Fossils are most often found within sedimentary rocks, which form on the Earth's surface as sediment accumulates in rivers, lakes and on the seafloor. The most common sedimentary rocks are sandstone, limestone and shale. You need to find somewhere where the bedrock is exposed (British Geological Survey maps can help). Coastal areas tend to be good places for the novice fossil hunter to start, as they're usually easily accessible.

Think of it as ancient wildlife watching. Although some people collect fossils we strongly recommend that you resist the urge to take them home. A fossil left in its rightful place will be enjoyed by people for years to come. Removing it could damage the fossil or the rock it's in. Record your find with your camera or sketchpad.

Fossil-finding hot spots

- The Jurassic Coast between Exmouth in East Devon and Studland Bay in Dorset is designated a World Heritage Site for rocks and fossils.
- Brownend Quarry, managed by Staffordshire Wildlife Trust, is important for its exposed rocks and fossils of the Lower Carboniferous period.
- The cliffs at Walton-on-the-Naze are one of the finest geological sites in Britain and are designated a Site of Special Scientific Interest. Essex Wildlife Trust owns a nature reserve next door.
- St Erth's Pits, managed by the Cornwall Wildlife Trust, contain the fossil evidence of ancient sea snails, sponges, corals, jellyfish, worms, sea squirts and fish.
- Don't collect fossils on nature reserves.

79.
WEATHER WATCH

Chatting about the weather is a commonplace activity for most Brits, but weather watching can also be gloriously wild.

Seeing a storm roll in off the sea or witnessing wind whipping leaves and cracking through woods and valleys is exciting and frightening. Phenomena like cloud inversion, when relatively warm rivers produce low-hanging steam clouds because the outside air is so bitterly cold, are weird and fantastical.

The keenest weather watchers could consider setting up a range of gadgets and gauges in their garden as a way of monitoring rainfall, wind speed and the like. A simple station with a rain gauge, weather vane and thermometer will help you gather some interesting data, or you could get more technical and buy an anemometer (to measure wind speed), a barometer (to measure pressure) and a hygrometer (to measure humidity). If you live somewhere for a long time, it can be really interesting monitoring patterns with your weather station. In an era of climate change, this is surely a more relevant activity than ever before.

80.
HABITATS: WOODLAND

Red and gold rustling leaves, weirdly shaped fungi, the smell of damp mosses... A walk through a wood on a bright autumnal day can bring joy to the heart. But the trees of our woodlands have a much deeper story to tell – one of fascinating creatures and ancient practices.

Our woodlands range from long-standing forests to modern plantations. So-called ancient woodlands have been under continuous tree cover for hundreds of years and often contain plants that are rarely found elsewhere, such as the unassuming herb-Paris. Different trees characterise our woodlands too. Broad-leaved woods are composed of deciduous trees, mixed woods of both deciduous and coniferous trees, and pine woods often of non-native trees planted for timber, until you reach the Caledonian pine forests of Scotland, home to the Scottish wildcat in the far north.

Woodlands come alive at dawn – tawny owls hoot to each other, while in spring wrens, blackcaps, warblers and nightingales fill the air with song. Great spotted woodpeckers, treecreepers and jays also visit broad-leaved and mixed woods, while goldcrests and rarer crossbills flit between the trees of conifer forests. Mammals like roe deer, foxes, red squirrels and dormice are regulars. And dead and rotting wood is important for fungi and insects like the impressively horned stag beetle.

But it's the spring flowers that our woodlands are really famous for. Carpets of bluebells herald the spring, when hoards of white ramsons fill the air with the exciting scent of garlic and pretty wood anemones and primroses line the paths.

Thousands of years of land management have dramatically reduced the UK's woodlands. But The Wildlife Trusts are managing many woodland nature reserves positively, using traditional techniques such as coppicing to encourage wildlife.

A Dorset Wildlife Trust
beach clean

81.
CLEAN UP YOUR COASTLINE

Britain's coastline is varied and dramatic, sometimes calm, sometimes wild, sometimes completely breathtaking. Some of the UK's wildest moments are to be had standing on top of remote coastal cliffs in the west of Wales or the deep south of Cornwall or the far northern Highlands.

Marine pollution is often invisible, but marine litter is a striking illustration of how polluted our seas really are. Our coastlines can be stunning but they can also be dirty and depressing. Walk along a single stretch of beach on a bad day and you could see thousands of cotton-bud sticks and cigarette butts.

There are 13,000 pieces of litter in every square kilometre of the world's oceans. Over 50% of that litter is plastic and its impact is deadly. Horrifyingly, far out in the Pacific Ocean there's a huge floating island of rubbish, nicknamed the Great Pacific Garbage Patch. It's a deadly mass of plastic bags, food wrappers and bottles that have floated there from all over the world. Marine animals can get tangled up in swirling litter and drown. Many have been found dead with stomachs full of rubbish. The Wildlife Trusts warn that 177 of our UK seabirds and animals are in danger because of plastic pollution.

Take action

- Never drop litter at the beach.
- Reduce and reuse waste, then recycle it.
- Pick up litter whenever you can.
- Join an organised coastal clean-up day.
- Volunteer for coastal Wildlife Trusts.

'Some of the UK's wildest moments are to be had standing on top of remote coastal cliffs'

82.
GO BLACKBERRYING

The most fun you can have in a hedgerow, blackberrying is the easiest and perhaps the most satisfying of all wild-food foraging. The fruits tend to appear in late summer, glorious dark purple berries that swarm over the bramble bushes lining many lanes and footpaths in the UK.

Keep an eye out for sites that look like they're going to get a high yield and make sure you're the first on the scene when the berries ripen. Armed with a large basket, and perhaps wearing old gloves to avoid scratches and something bright if you're picking on roadsides, a mere half-hour's blackberrying could result in a pound or more of fruit. Free food and utterly delicious.

Take the fruit home, give it a wash and then use it in fruit salads, jams and pies. But do make sure you leave some behind for wildlife to enjoy too. Blackberries are enjoyed by birds, butterflies and some mammals.

83.
TAKE WILD PHOTOGRAPHS

Wildlife photography is an art and certain pictures can stop you in your tracks, leaving you awestruck at both the beauty of the subject and also the skill of the photographer. The professionals spend years mastering their techniques, with amazing results, but armed with a decent digital camera, some patience and creativity, you can successfully photograph UK wildlife, which is as varied and interesting as anything you'd find on safari.

A few photography tips

- **RESEARCH YOUR SUBJECT:** the more you know about a species or a habitat, the more likely you are to capture it at its most interesting or aesthetically pleasing moment.

- **OBSERVE:** spending time in the field and watching the wildlife you want to shoot is crucial. Get to know your subject, visit at different times of day and during different seasons to witness its many guises.

- **USE A TRIPOD WHERE POSSIBLE:** it will help you get steady shots. If you're filming rather than photographing, a tripod is essential.

- **THINK ABOUT THE LIGHT:** play with it and use it to create different effects. Be aware that different times of day will affect the type of picture you get.

- **TRY NEW ANGLES:** don't do the obvious. Try photographing things from interesting angles and challenging new perspectives.

- **EXPERIMENT:** cameras are toys after all and should be played with.

- **BE PATIENT AND BE LUCKY:** wildlife doesn't perform on demand. If you want to take great pictures you're probably going to do a fair bit of waiting around.

- **THINK ABOUT THE WILDLIFE:** remember, do not disturb or harm any wild animals while trying to photograph them. Also, it is illegal to take photographs of wild birds and their nests without a special licence.

Stag at dawn

84.
WATCH SUNRISE

Dawn belongs to the animals. When you rise with the sun, or stay up until it arrives, the land is dew soaked and wildlife uninhibited. The air is crisper and cleaner, noises are natural rather than man-made and everything smells different. The sun is weak and the light is hazy.

This is the time of day to listen to birds and watch foxes. It's the time of day to walk through wet fields and stand silently and stare. Go to a west-facing beach just before dawn cracks, wrap yourself in a blanket and watch the sun tease the sky, gradually nudging higher and higher and bathing everything in morning light.

85.
BUILD A POND

Ponds greatly improve a garden's wildlife potential. Even small ponds can support a rich diversity of wildlife and provide places for animals to bathe, drink and mate. A series of ponds in a neighbourhood creates essential corridors and networks of wildlife habitat. Ponds also store carbon, helping to reduce the impact of climate change.

The first things to consider are location, shape and size. The best place is a level sunny spot away from trees, shade, roots and leaf fall. Dappled shade won't be a problem. Ponds with natural, undulating shapes have longer edges and greater value for wildlife. When it comes to buying a liner, a flexible one is more sustainable than a pre-moulded or concrete liner and creates a better habitat for wildlife. Flexible liners made from butyl are expensive but hard-wearing.

How to do it

1. Mark out your chosen shape with string, a hose pipe or a line of sand.
2. Dig out the shape to a depth of about 60 cm. Start at the edge and work in. Save any turf to place along the edge of the pond later.
3. Create sloping sides that support a range of plants and will allow animals to get in and out easily.
4. Create varied shallow margins from 1–25 cm to suit different marginal plants. This area will be warmer and encourage frogs and toads to spawn. It will also be a stable edge for mammals to drink from.
5. Vary the profile. You can create soil shelves as you dig or build ledges from rocks or stones after you have laid your liner.
6. Add a shallower boggy area near the pond edge for species to migrate into.
7. Before you lay the liner, remove roots, stones and rubble and firm the soil down.
8. Cover the hole with a 3-cm layer of builder's sand followed by an underliner, such as a polyester sheet or old carpet.

9. Starting at one edge, unroll the liner across your pond.
10. Make sure the liner overlaps the edges of the pond by about 30 cm. Secure it in place with rocks or bricks.
11. Cut any excess liner and tuck the edges under varied materials, such as stones, a pebble beach, large flat rocks, turf, logs or paving slabs.
12. Cover the liner with a thin layer of sieved soil and, if possible, add some soil from an established pond.
13. Fill the pond with water, ideally rainwater collected in a water butt. The water will press the liner into shape.

'Ponds with natural, undulating shapes have longer edges and greater value for wildlife'

Planting

Aquatic plants oxygenate a pond and help to keep the water clean. They also provide food, shelter, shade and breeding and nesting places. Wait ten days to allow the water and soil to settle before introducing plants. Use varied plants suited to the different depths.

Keeping it wild

- Keep the grass long around the edge of your pond to provide places for animals to shelter.
- If your pond freezes, make holes in the ice to allow frogs and other animals to breathe.
- Provide long grass and piles of stones or logs close to the pond for animals to shelter in over winter.
- Don't introduce frogs or other amphibians from other ponds because this can spread disease.
- Don't add fish because they will eat smaller animals such as mayfly larvae.

Common Tern

86.
VISIT HILTON GRAVEL PITS

Derby and Burton Upon Trent,
Derbyshire and Staffordshire

This watery reserve is a perfect place to pond dip, as well as see a range of fascinating wildlife, from dragonflies to black poplar trees. Make sure you bring a net and visit the pond-dipping platform.

What will you see?

These former gravel pits are now flooded, providing perfect conditions for wildlife, particularly dragonflies and damselflies in the summer. The reserve attracts 15 species, including the magnificent emperor dragonfly and the jewel-like emerald damselfly. The wetlands are also a great place for amphibians to breed and you may see the protected great crested newt as well as frogs and toads.

A tern raft on the main lagoon attracts breeding common terns in the summer, while many other birds visit the reserve throughout the year,

Pond dipping

> *'Patient observation may also be*
> *rewarded with the spectacular sight*
> *of a kingfisher diving for fish'*

from other waterfowl, like teals and mallards, to smaller birds, such as bullfinches, willow tits and long-tailed tits. Patient observation may also be rewarded with the spectacular sight of a kingfisher diving for fish. The information panel on site will give you handy tips and a species identification guide.

RESERVE NAME: Hilton Gravel Pits
GRID REF: SK249315
NEAREST TOWN: Derby / Burton Upon Trent
WILDLIFE TRUST: Derbyshire Wildlife Trust
WEBSITE: www.derbyshirewildlifetrust.org.uk
CONTACT: 01773 881188 / enquiries@derbyshirewt.co.uk
TRANSPORT: Burton Upon Trent, Willington and Derby stations; parking adjacent to the site
OTHER RESERVES NEARBY: Willington Gravel Pits (SK285274)

87.
KEEP BEES

Keeping bees is quite a commitment but the rewards are great: not just a personal supply of fresh, local honey but also your own home-grown honeycomb and beeswax. It's a wildlife-friendly pursuit as well. Bees are not just nice to have around and providers of honey for our toast, they're crucial to agriculture. Bees are worth millions to British farming, relied upon to pollinate at least a third of the food we eat.

Only four types of UK bee actually make honey, but all species have a vital role to play in the ecosystem, pollinating our food crops and flowers. Nearly all of our 250 species of bee are in decline and honeybee numbers have fallen by 10–15% in the last two years alone. Keeping bees is a way of maintaining strong colonies that can help build up resistance to disease.

Urbanites especially have been embracing the beekeeping way of life, with working hives now found in gardens and on rooftops across sprawling cities such as London. Stylish new beehive designs are helping to keep things simple and chic. Some people even think city bees actually tend to produce tastier honey, as they usually have a more diverse range of plants and flowers to collect nectar from.

Not only delicious, honey is good for you too! Full of natural sugars, a spoonful of honey is a far healthier way of sweetening drinks and baking than using refined sugar. A dollop of honey in a hot lemony drink, possibly with a nip of whisky too, is the only good thing about having a cold. Hay fever sufferers swear by locally produced honey as a way of keeping their symptoms under control.

Beekeepers need to buy a hive and select the type of bees they want to keep. They need specialist clothing and equipment, like a suit, a veil, a smoker and a honey extractor. If you're serious you should definitely enrol on a course – wherever you live there will be a local beekeepers' association not far away, on hand to offer all the assistance and advice you need.

88.
FORAGE

If you get to know your fruits, fungi and flora well enough, a whole new edible landscape can open up before your eyes. Some of the tastiest treats you could try foraging for include elderflowers, blackberries, chestnuts and stinging nettles. Or perhaps you could collect ingredients for a small salad of ramsons (wild garlic), sorrel, watercress and salad burnet.

Dedicated foragers say that, as long as you respect the countryside and collect food in a sustainable way, foraging is a great way to connect with and understand the natural world.

You don't have to eat everything you find though. It could easily be argued that it's just as satisfying to forage for fungi, see it in its natural surroundings and then simply walk on and leave it for other people to enjoy and wildlife to eat. If everyone starts tucking in, there won't be anything left! You also have to be incredibly careful – some mushrooms, plants and fruits are highly poisonous and can kill.

If you're keen to have a go, why not seek out a foraging course or guided walk in the first instance? Some Wildlife Trusts and other groups organise wild-food sessions and bushcraft activities, which often include making a fire and cooking up a feast as well.

89.
MULCH YOUR GARDEN

Mulching is a simple way to make your garden more wildlife friendly and climate proof. Mulch provides cover for small animals, and, as it breaks down, it enriches the soil and nourishes plants and animals. This, in turn, will encourage even more wildlife into your garden. Adding a thick layer of organic mulch to your soil is one of the easiest and most useful jobs you can do to reduce the severity of climate change. It regulates soil temperature, reduces the need to water, suppresses weeds and helps to prevent soil erosion.

Home-made mulch is ideal but you could also seek some out at your local stables or buy some from a good garden centre. Check its colour and consistency to ensure it's top quality. The best mulch comes from well-rotted, natural and organic material – things like horse manure, garden compost or leaf mould.

Well-rotted compost should be a rich colour; it should crumble easily when handled and be moist but not too wet. You shouldn't be able to identify what the mulch was made from – if you can, then it hasn't rotted down enough and may leach nutrients from the soil and 'burn' tender plants. The best time to mulch is when the soil is fairly wet in late autumn and again in spring. If you can only mulch once, do it in spring to prepare your soil for a dry summer.

How to mulch

1. Fork in or rake off any excess mulch from the previous season that hasn't broken down into the soil.

2. If your soil is dry, first use a watering can to moisten the ground.

3. Spread the mulch in a layer 5 to 10 cm thick around plants and trees.

4. Make sure you leave a mulch-free gap of 5 cm around trees and larger stems.

5. Don't add mulch on top of emerging growth and tender new seedlings.

90.
TAKE A SPORE PRINT

Taking a spore print is a method of identifying wild mushrooms, but it's also rather good fun and results in some pretty pictures to stick on your fridge door.

First you will need to remove the stem from your mushroom so you are left with just the cap. Place the cap gill-side down on your paper and cover it with a bowl to protect it from drafts and prevent it drying out. Leave the cap for several hours or even overnight, then remove the bowl, gently peel the cap away from the paper and admire the spore print it leaves behind.

Make sure you wash your hands – the fungi you find out and about could easily be poisonous. It's always worth having a decent mushroom guide so you have more of an idea about what you're dealing with.

Common and magnificently named UK fungi

- Amethyst deceiver
- Beefsteak fungus
- Collared earthstar
- Dryad's saddle (pictured)
- Giant puffball
- Glistening ink cap
- Milking bonnet
- Stinkhorn
- Wood blewit
- Woolly milk cap

91.
VISIT THE ERCALL
Wellington, Telford, Shropshire

A huge chunk was blasted out of this hillside to provide road stone for the nearby M54. This was certainly destructive, but it had the unexpectedly wonderful effect of laying bare the earth's history, revealing rocks from the earliest beginnings of life on this planet and creating a nature reserve that teems with life.

What will you see?

The Ercall is a place where you can travel in time. If you look at the exposed rock you'll see ripples in the surface where waves lapped on an ancient shoreline some 500 million years ago. Amazingly, this part of Britain used to be 60 degrees south of the equator – try to imagine that, standing there on a wet, wintry day!

Study the giant pink and grey rock face and look back in time to the point where life exploded across the face of the earth. The pink rock is like granite, born of fire and once molten hot lava; the grey rock is sandstone, made on a white, sandy beach. This change in rock marks a change in Shropshire from volcanic violence to shallow seas, and a time when life flourished in these seas. The fossils left behind bring ancient wildlife ever closer to our understanding.

It's not just old rocks that make the Ercall interesting, though. In spring the woods are awash with bluebells and the song of birds just returned

RESERVE NAME: The Ercall
GRID REF: SJ644095
NEAREST TOWN: Wellington, Telford
WILDLIFE TRUST: Shropshire Wildlife Trust
WEBSITE: www.shropshirewildlifetrust.org.uk
CONTACT: 01743 284280 / email via the website
TRANSPORT: Wellington train station; parking at nearby Forest Glen
OTHER RESERVES NEARBY: Granville Country Park (SJ719132)

CLOCKWISE FROM TOP LEFT
The Ercall • Bluebell Carpet • Dingy Skipper

from Africa, while in summer plentiful bird's-foot trefoil makes this a favoured stronghold of one of Telford's best loved butterflies, the dingy skipper.

A recent survey of the nature reserve's invertebrates (butterflies, beetles, spiders, bees, bugs and ants) yielded a staggering 821 species. It's also an excellent place to look for fungi in the autumn, as well as to enjoy the changing colours sweeping through the ancient oak woodland.

Things you should know

- The nature reserve used to be part of a quarry, so while the path is fairly wide and surfaced with old tarmac and compacted gravel, after heavy rain it can be difficult to negotiate. Parts of the reserve can become very muddy and getting up into the woodland means going up some long, fairly steep slopes.
- Climb the Wrekin, the Ercall's big sister. This iconic West Midlands hill is right next door to the Ercall. Simply park at the Forest Glen and then walk up the challenging path to the summit, where spectacular views across Shropshire and beyond await.

92.
MAKE BLACKBERRY JAM

Is there anything finer than a hot crumpet slathered with home-made jam? Perhaps, but not much. It's actually really easy to make your own and it's a way to put the fruits of all your blackberrying labours to good use. The key to this is starting to collect empty jam jars well in advance of your jam-making session, otherwise you'll have an awful lot of conserve and nowhere to put it.

If you want pipless jam, you'll need to stew the two fruits separately and then put the stewed blackberries through a very fine sieve or squeeze them through muslin. Once sieved, put the two fruits together, add the sugar and boil as usual.

You will need ...

- Blackberries
- Half the weight of the blackberries in cooking apples
- White granulated sugar
- Sterilised jam jars and lids
- Greaseproof paper
- Labels

How to do it

1. Wash the blackberries in cold water. Pick out any that look a bit mouldy and evict any live inhabitants.

2. Peel, core and roughly chop the apples.

3. Put the fruit into a covered bowl and cook in a microwave until it's soft – the timing will depend on how much fruit you have. Check it every four minutes.

4. When the fruit is soft and runny – there will be a lot of juice – pour it into a measuring jug to find out how much you've got.

5. Pour the fruit into a large pan and add 340–450 g of sugar for each pint of fruit, depending how sweet you like your jam.

6. Bring the fruit and sugar quickly to the boil and then simmer until it starts to set.

7. Test a drop on a cold spoon. If the drop stiffens and quickly forms a skin, it's ready. If not, keep cooking the mixture until it is.

8. Pour the hot jam into hot jam jars that have been sterilised. You can sterilise the clean jars by filling them with boiling water. Make sure the jars are already warm or they will crack.

9. Cover the jam, while still hot, with circles of greaseproof paper.

10. Leave to cool and then put on the lids, or use the traditional circle of gingham fabric and an elastic band. Stick on a label, detailing the type of jam and the date it was made.

11. Store in the fridge.

93. HABITATS:
RIVER AND STREAM

The UK's waterways range from small, shallow ponds and tiny, trickling streams to lengthy, gushing rivers, like the Severn and Thames. With such a variety of flow patterns, channels and meanders, coupled with a whole range of different bank habitats, rivers and streams support a diverse range of plants and animals. Riffles and pools support aquatic species, while exposed sediments, like shingle beds, are important for invertebrates. Rivers and streams also provide wildlife with 'corridors' which they can use to move between fragmented habitats.

Our waterways support many species of fish including brown trout, eel, stickleback, pike, grayling, roach, perch and salmon. Charismatic otters patrol the riverbanks at night, leaving clues to their presence for wildlife detectives, such as scats and footprints. Other iconic waterside wildlife include water voles, whose presence is sometimes betrayed by a neat plop, or the metallic flash of a kingfisher whizzing past.

There are few rivers in the UK that we haven't had an impact upon. Canalisation and tree removal has led to bank erosion, pollution has caused the devastation of species, dam and reservoir construction has changed water flows and the introduction of invasive plants and animals has had terrible effects. Added to this, our floodplains – natural places where rivers can deluge their loads after heavy rains – are threatened by development.

But there is hope. We have started to recognise that healthy wetlands are important, not just for wildlife, but also to help prevent flooding. River and floodplain restoration projects carried out by The Wildlife Trusts are aiding these vital habitats.

94.
MAKE A DEN IN
VIKING WOODS

Preston, Lancashire

Penwortham Education Centre has woodland, a wildlife garden, a variety of ponds, mature hedgerows, a drystone wall and a wild-flower meadow, not to mention a Viking longhouse!

What will you see?

In spring you can see frogs and newts and the beautiful flowers of the snake's head fritillary, while the Viking Woods are carpeted with bluebells and wild garlic.

The main attraction of the reserve is the programme of school-holiday activities for children and families. Penwortham runs all kinds of events – from pond dipping and beast hunts, to environ-mental art and bush craft, to survival skills. Go and make a den, get creative with clay and natural materials, or see how many different creatures you can discover in the pond.

Things you should know

- Phone ahead and book on to a special Wild Side activity day or a family day.
- There's disabled access, toilets, indoor classrooms and parking. There's also a small shop and indoor and outdoor picnic areas.

RESERVE NAME: Penwortham Environment Education Centre
NEAREST TOWN: Preston
WILDLIFE TRUST: Lancashire, Manchester and North Merseyside Wildlife Trust
WEBSITE: www.lancswt.org.uk
CONTACT: 01772 751110 / info@lancswt.org.uk
TRANSPORT: Preston railway station; parking on site
OTHER RESERVES NEARBY: Mere Sands Wood (SD447157)

95.
READ ANIMAL TRACKS AND SIGNS

It's not just elusive and rare animals that are rarely seen by most of us. Lots of relatively common and widespread species avoid contact with people and live lifestyles that prove difficult for us to follow. To get a real idea of the wildlife around us, we may need to deploy a few naturalist's tricks to discover the real lives of our wild neighbours.

With some detective work, you can investigate identities, solve mysteries and murders, reveal nocturnal activity and plot the boundaries of territories, simply by learning to interpret the tracks and signs that are all around. You may find evidence of more wildlife than you'd expect. Next time you're out and about, take a closer look for these clues, because you might never know what's out there...

Feeding signs

Where birds have met an unfortunate end at the hands of a predator, look closely at the scattering of freshly pulled feathers and you ❯❯

might identify the culprit. Feather shafts with their pointed ends intact suggest removal by plucking, indicating a bird of prey such as a sparrowhawk. Roughly chewed ends are the work of a toothed enemy such as a fox.

Owl pellets contain the undigested bones and fur of prey and are the perfect receipt of a recent meal. Chewed nut casings reveal the identity of the diner by the shape of the hole and tooth marks left. De-scaled pine cones are the work of squirrels, as is gnawed bark on high tree branches. Stripping closer to the ground suggests deer or rabbits.

Footprints

Mud and snow provide the ideal medium for impressions of the animals roaming our countryside. Look for the five toes, squat palm and long, strong claws of the badger. The four pads of fox prints closely resemble domestic dogs but are narrower in shape, often creating a neat, straight line rather than the staggered gait of the dog. The two tiny slots of muntjac deer are easily distinguished from their larger cousins, with the pointed end indicating the direction of travel.

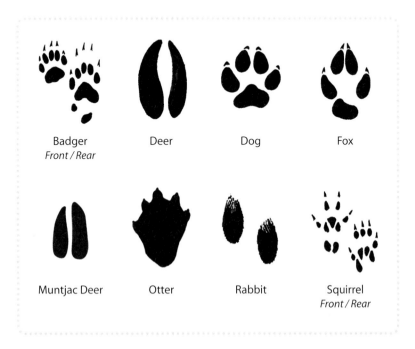

Badger
Front / Rear

Deer

Dog

Fox

Muntjac Deer

Otter

Rabbit

Squirrel
Front / Rear

Homes and roosts

The spraints of fox and otter mark wandering territories, and well worn paths through grass often lead to holes, dens and badger setts. Use guano and droppings to find the roosts of birds and bats and the raised earth of molehills to reveal underground tunnels. Bundles of twigs high in tree branches could be squirrel dreys or bird nests, and neatly woven grasses at ground level may hint at mice.

96.
GO CRABBING
(The wildlife friendly way)

Rockpools and mudflats are perfect places to find crabs, but remember that however hard they might look on the outside they're really soft on the inside, so be gentle with them.

You will need ...

- A fishing line
- A mesh bag, like you get with laundry tablets, or citrus fruit
- A net
- A large bucket
- Bait – bacon, cheese and fish all work, but never use limpets or other wildlife as bait

How to do it

1. Tie the mesh bag on to the line. Put the bait into the bag.
2. Dangle the line into the water and when a crab finds the bait put the net under it and carefully pull it up.
3. Put the crab in the bucket. Don't mix small and big crabs because they'll fight, and don't put more than three crabs in one bucket.
4. For a closer look, use your thumb and forefinger and gently pick the crab up from the back at widest part of the shell.
5. Don't keep the crabs out of the water for long and release them gently back where you found them.

97.
VISIT PURBECK MARINE WILDLIFE RESERVE

Wareham, Dorset

Kimmeridge Bay, in the Purbeck Marine Wildlife Reserve, has long been a favourite destination of divers and rock-poolers, but it's also the perfect place for snorkelling, and in recent years more and more people have been taking advantage of the often crystal-clear waters to admire the amazing variety of marine life.

What will you see?

Underwater, the huge assortment of seaweeds create a colourful backdrop, from the carpets of pink coral weed and vibrant blue rainbow wrack to the impressive stands of golden bootlace and sargassum seaweed. The seabed offers a wide range of habitats for a multitude of inhabitants: white sandy patches reflect sunlight on to shimmering shoals of sand eels, while rocky reefs provide cover for all manner of crustaceans, including red-eyed velvet swimming crabs, spiny spider crabs and even the occasional lobster.

An underwater snorkel trail is laid in Kimmeridge Bay from May to September each year, when the water in the bay is usually a degree or two higher than the open sea. May and June are best for colourful seaweeds and the possibility of seeing mating sea hares, cuttlefish and nesting corkwing wrasse. In August and September the water is at its warmest, and though the seaweeds have lost a lot of their colour in the strong sunlight, the bay becomes an ideal nursery area for juvenile fish, such as pollack, bib and mullet. It's also home to surprisingly large ballan wrasse and the occasional predatory sea bass.

The 400 m trail is best dived during neap tides, at the time of half-moon when the tide is weakest. It has a maximum depth of 3.5 m, although much of it is little more than standing depth. A waterproof ID guide directs the snorkeller around the five

numbered buoys and explains what to look out for. These, along with underwater cameras, are available to buy from the Fine Foundation Marine Centre, where the wardens are always interested to hear what marine life you have seen.

Things you should know

- In rough weather the water is much less clear and little will be seen, so check tides, visibility and sea conditions before you travel.
- It is important to respect the wildlife in the Purbeck Marine Wildlife Reserve and follow the Snorkeller's Code.
- The trail is only suitable for adults and children who are confident swimmers and confident in the sea. There's no disabled access.

RESERVE NAME: Purbeck Marine Wildlife Reserve
GRID REF: SY909787
NEAREST TOWN: Kimmeridge, Wareham, Dorset
WILDLIFE TRUST: Dorset Wildlife Trust
WEBSITE: www.dorsetwildlifetrust.org.uk
CONTACT: 01929 481044 / kimmeridge@dorsetwildlifetrust.org.uk
TRANSPORT: Wareham train station; parking on site (£4). No public transport to Kimmeridge
OTHER RESERVES NEARBY: Kilwood (SY937827), Stonehill Down (SY925822), Tadnoll (SY792873) and Winfrith (SY805870)

98.
EXPLORE A WILD ORCHARD

Orchards across the UK are being recognised as vital wildlife refuges. They often contain a mosaic of habitats – trees, scrub, hedgerow and grassland – that can support a wide range of wildlife. They recently became a national priority habitat under the UK Biodiversity Action Plan, a blueprint for protecting wildlife.

Autumn is a great time to visit an orchard. In preparation for the cold months ahead, mammals, bats and birds feast on fallen fruit and insects attracted to the fruit. Fungi, like wax caps, giant puff-

> *'Orchards across the UK are being recognised as vital wildlife refuges'*

balls, field mushrooms and bracket fungus, emerge on the orchard floor or tree trunks. A seasonal favourite, mistletoe is our only native white-berried plant. It's spread by the mistle thrush and is semi-parasitic, often found on apple trees. It's a great source of food for birds during winter.

Perhaps not the most obvious thing to actively seek out, orchards are also fantastic places for some serious moss and lichen spotting. Stand back from a tree and see how many hues of lichen you can see. From the bright-orange Xanthoria parientina to the apple-green Flavoparmelia caperata to the grey, leafy Parmotrema perlatum, there's a whole rainbow of lichens to discover.

Orchards that are sensitively managed for both fruit and wildlife will have a greater richness and diversity of insects, which means a much higher ratio of useful insects to pests, as well as a greater number of pollinators. By using fewer chemicals, and including a range of other native plants, natural predators like ladybirds and hoverflies will be attracted and help to prevent and reduce pest problems. Crucial pollinators like bees and wasps will benefit from an orchard floor covered in nectar-rich wild flowers, while many species of invertebrates depend on the dead wood in old orchards.

Remember: don't pick apples from a nature reserve and don't pick apples from someone's land without permission.

Where to find wild orchards

- Clattinger Farm, Wiltshire
- Broad Oak Orchard, Dorset
- The Knapp and Papermill, Worcestershire
- Martin's Meadows, Suffolk
- Tewin Orchard, Hertfordshire
- Throughout Wiltshire, where a traditional orchards project is currently investigating the county's 500 orchards

99.
VISIT FOLLY FARM

Bristol, Avon

Sandwiched between Bristol and Bath, Folly Farm is a 101-hectare nature reserve overlooking Chew Valley Lake. A little piece of history tucked away in the Mendips, it was once a ferme ornée (ornamental farm) for the Sutton Court Estate, which was never farmed intensively.

What will you see?

Walking through the ancient woodland of Folly Wood in spring, you'll hear the clamour of newly arrived blackcaps and chiffchaffs as you wind your way through a carpet of bluebells, ramsons and stands of early purple orchids. Ascend to the ridge of Round Hill in summer and you'll see buzzards soar on the surrounding thermals with the backdrop of the Chew Valley behind them.

Roe deer may be spotted in the maturing plantation and, in high summer, the hay meadows at the top of the ridge are filled with wild flowers like purple knapweed and devil's-bit scabious, both feeding plants for clouds of butterflies. In the early evening badgers can be seen by patient watchers on the circular Access Trail.

In autumn the brambles along the edge of the pastures of East Hill are laden with blackberries. Red admiral and peacock butterflies feed here and stockpiles of conkers are nibbled by short-tailed voles in the hedgerow. The ghostly shape of a barn owl quartering the meadow beside the woodland is a common sight on early winter afternoons.

RESERVE NAME: Folly Farm
GRID REF: ST610603
NEAREST TOWN: Bristol
WILDLIFE TRUST: Avon Wildlife Trust
WEBSITE: www.follyfarm.org
CONTACT: 0117 917 7270 /
mail@avonwildlifetrust.org.uk
TRANSPORT: Bristol Temple Meads and Bath Spa
railway stations; parking on site

100.
LEARN THE DIFFERENCE BETWEEN CRICKETS AND GRASSHOPPERS

Cricket   Grasshopper

SIZE: Crickets tend to be smaller than grasshoppers.

ANTENNAE: Crickets have very long antennae whereas grasshoppers don't.

MOVEMENT: Grasshoppers can jump and fly but although some crickets can fly and jump, they often prefer to walk away from trouble.

ACTIVITY: Grasshoppers tend to be more active during the day, whereas crickets are more nocturnal creatures (although you can hear them during the day, mostly in the evening).

COLOUR: Grasshoppers tend to be duller shades of green and brown whereas crickets can be quite brightly-coloured.

CERCI: Crickets have particularly long 'cerci' – tail-like projections at the rear of their body. Grasshoppers have them too but they are generally smaller. Some female crickets have a particularly fearsome-looking ovipositor (egg laying tube).

FOOD: Grasshoppers feed mainly on grass. Crickets mostly feed on bits of animals.

Where to find them

The best place to look for grasshoppers and crickets is a grassland nature reserve in the summer. Ask your local Wildlife Trust or check their website for details of where to go.

101.
MAKE AN INSECT HOTEL

Attract insects to your garden by providing them with valuable habitats: make like a minibeast property magnate and build them a hotel. You can go for the express version or try creating something a little bit more deluxe.

The Insect Express

- Hollow plant stems, like bamboo canes
- Twigs and sticks
- String

How to do it

1. Collect handfuls of stems, twigs and sticks.
2. Tie the bundles quite tightly in two places.
3. Post the bundle into a hedge or hang in a sheltered place, perhaps from a bushy tree.
4. For a different kind of look, you could stuff the sticks into a flower pot.

The Insect Deluxe

- Small logs or untreated timber
- Hollow plant stems, like bamboo canes
- Twigs and sticks
- A wood saw
- Nails and a hammer or a screwdriver and wood screws
- A drill and 5 mm wood bit
- Wire

How to do it

1. Make a wooden frame, fixing the wood with screws or nails.
2. Fill the frame with stems, twigs and sticks.
3. Fix a wire loop to the back of the frame and hang somewhere sheltered.

102.
WALK ATOP A CLIFF

Coastal cliff-top walks are frequently breathtaking, offering sweeping views of craggy landscapes giving way to roaring ocean. Headlands are perfect for watching sea birds and marine creatures. They're also home to interesting and hardy plants – maritime grassland species like pink thrift, delicate white sea campion and sea plantain, and heathland species like heather, gorse and bracken. You might also see things like climbing corydalis or buck's horn plantain, or perhaps the foodie-sounding sea pea, wild asparagus or oyster plant.

A few cliff-top reserves

- Cemaes Head, Pembrokeshire
- Flamborough Cliffs, Yorkshire
- Handa Island, Highlands and Skye
- Humphrey Head, Cumbria
- Phillips Point, Cornwall
- Redley Cliff, Glamorgan
- Sandwich and Pegwell Bay, Kent
- Vau du Saou, Alderney

103.
COUNT CROCUSES AT LLANMEREWIG GLEBE

Llanmerewig Glebe, Montgomeryshire

A chance to see the rare Autumn Crocus in full flower.

What will you see?

Llanmerewig Glebe is an example of a lowland meadow, an increasingly rare habitat, which is home to an impressive list of plant species including Imperforate St John's-wort and Devil's-bit Scabious. The reserve is surrounded by ancient, species-rich hedgerows offering shelter to chiffchaff, willow warbler and long-tailed tit.

The reserve is also home to a rare colony of Meadow Saffron – known as Autumn Crocus – whose leaves and flowers are poisonous! The plant still thrives here probably because the meadow has been farmed traditionally for years, providing rich hay crops and late autumn grazing, though animals are not put on the field until the Autumn Crocus has finished flowering. Visit in September, when the Meadow Saffron is in full flower. Every year, the Montgomeryshire Wildlife Trust run an event to count the number of flowers in bloom – sometimes as many as 1000! This annual count is a popular event and helps the Trust monitor the status of the Meadow Saffron.

RESERVE NAME: Llanmerewig Glebe
GRID REF: SO 160930
NEAREST TOWN: Abermule
WILDLIFE TRUST: Montgomeryshire Wildlife Trust
WEBSITE: www.montwt.co.uk
CONTACT: 01938 555654 / info@montwt.co.uk
TRANSPORT: Welshpool railway station
OTHER RESERVES NEARBY: Pwll Penarth (SO 137926),
Red House (SO 170968) and Dolydd Hafren (SJ 208005)

104.
STARGAZE

The North Star, also called Polaris, has been used by navigators for hundreds of years. Bright and signposting north it is probably the most famous star in the sky but it's a common misconception that it's the brightest. A different star, Sirius, can lay claim to this.

Finding the North Star

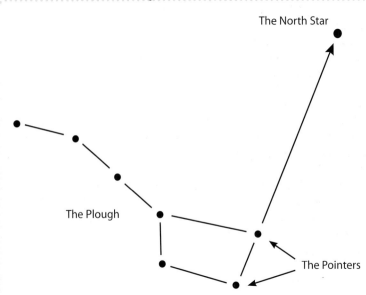

1. **Find the Plough.** It rotates in the sky, so is not always the same way up but it keeps the same shape.
2. Look for two stars called the Pointers at one end of the Plough.
3. Use your fingers to calculate the distance between the Pointers.
4. Then look for a star that is five times that distance in the direction that the Pointers show.
5. The North Star is not the brightest, but it is on its own so is usually fairly easy to spot.

105. HABITATS: URBAN WASTELAND

Wildlife is often more resilient than we give it credit for. It can thrive in the most unexpected places, including on industrial wastelands where old factories, housing, docks or power stations crumble, or railway sidings and roadsides go to ruin.

The term 'wasteland' has negative connotations, implying land of no environmental, social or economic value. But in terms of wildlife, these can be areas of great importance in the urban landscape. Whether colonised naturally or helped a little along the way, the diversity of species wasteland or 'brownfield' sites can support is surprising. Not only that, but these areas, so often seen as derelict and useless, can form important corridors for wildlife, linking up other natural habitats nearby.

The open character of some of these areas, with their disturbed soils and bare patches, makes them excellent for invertebrates and reptiles. Lizards can be spotted basking in the sun, while slow worms shelter under old tin. Garden plants colonise easily: buddleia attracting peacock and tortoiseshell butterflies. And specialised wildlife may come to find a home too. The black redstart relishes life on brownfield sites so much that conservationists in London are looking to replace those sites that eventually get developed by creating similar habitats on nearby roofs!

Railways and roadsides can support a variety of plants. In chalky areas, wild marjoram, ox-eye daisy, broom and kidney vetch make their home on cutting slopes, while on clay soils goat's beard, cow parsley and ivy flourish.

Wastelands often disappear under new development, however, so The Wildlife Trusts are working with developers and planners to provide guidance on the management of these unique habitats.

106.
BUILD A TREE HOUSE

Tree houses are absolutely magical and in an ideal world everyone would have one, but building one is quite a project, requiring time, cash and also some serious thought when it comes to safety. You don't want to build a palace among the branches that ends up being a death trap. It may well be much more fun to design your dream hideaway and then call in the experts to do the hard work.

A few things to consider ...

- First, you need a large tree in which the house can be constructed. Decide how big you want your house to be and whether you want it to be visible or hidden. Do your neighbours need to be consulted?

- Think about how you're going to access the house and, more pressingly at this stage, how you're going to physically build something up a tree if you're set on doing it yourself. A decent ladder will definitely be needed. Safety harnesses, ropes, pulleys and the like may also be required.

- Think about the elements, where the sun is, how exposed the site is. How does the tree change over the seasons?

- A sturdy platform is the key to successful tree-house construction. It should be built close to the trunk and preferably supported by branches or posts. It needs to be level and able to withstand uneven loads. It shouldn't sway.

- Next you can make a floor on top of the platform, perhaps using exterior graded plywood or even proper floorboards. And then build walls and a roof. These could be built in situ or put together on solid ground and then hauled into place. Weatherproof the roof with felt or thatch.

- Securely attach a ladder or rope to the tree to make getting up and down from the house easy. It may be worth making the area at the bottom of the tree extra soft in case of missed footings. A cushioning layer of bark chippings would work well.

- You should make regular safety inspections of the tree house, especially after each winter.

107.
BASK IN A HAZE OF PURPLE HEATHER

Ruthin, Denbighshire, North Wales

Surrounded by glorious panoramic views and located alongside a lake, Gors Maen Llwyd is an upland heathland reserve with blanket-bog habitat. The Welsh name means 'Bog of the Grey Stone', referring to a glacial erratic – a piece of rock from another place and time – carried by a great ice sheet and left behind at the end of the last ice age. It's a great place to go and bask in a purple haze of heather.

What will you see?

Gors Maen Llwyd is a fantastic way to experience 280 hectares of wild Wales at any time of year, but it is not to be missed when the heather is in bloom in late summer.

The reserve hosts a Bronze Age round-house site and burial mounds, or 'tumuli', which, before the valley was flooded to create Llyn Brenig reservoir, would have been prominent on the hillside. A ruined shepherd's cottage (late 1800s) also hints at the reserve's past.

In the early dawn of a spring day, black grouse can be heard 'lekking' (a common mating ritual for the species) on the site. Mad march hares might also put on a display for springtime visitors. The warmer months bring an abundance of insects that provide food for many birds, including black and red grouse.

RESERVE NAME: Gors Maen Llwyd
GRID REF: SH975 580
NEAREST TOWN: Ruthin
WILDLIFE TRUST: North Wales Wildlife Trust
WEBSITE: www.northwaleswildlifetrust.org.uk
CONTACT: 01248 351541 / nwwt@wildlifetrustswales.org
TRANSPORT: The reserve is seven miles south-west of Denbigh. Park at the top car park (SH970580) or near the bird hide (SH9835754)

The reserve comes into its own in the late summer and early autumn with an awesome display of purple heather. Further splashes of colour come from golden bog asphodel, delicate blue harebells and cranberries, crowberries and bilberries. From the lake shore you can watch goosanders, great crested grebes and cormorants feeding on fish, and sand martins nesting in the sandy banks.

Things you should know

- Paths are unsurfaced and uneven in places and the weather on the moors can be unpredictable – stout footwear and waterproofs are recommended.
- Many of the moorland birds nest on the ground and are therefore easily disturbed during the nesting season, so be careful in the spring and summer. Stick to paths and keep dogs under control.

108.
VISIT GIBRALTAR POINT NATIONAL NATURE RESERVE
Skegness, Lincolnshire

Gibraltar Point is famous as a wild, unspoilt coastline, stretching from the southern end of Skegness to the mouth of Britain's largest estuary, the Wash. With over 400 hectares of windswept sand dunes, expanses of creek-dissected saltmarsh, meadows and freshwater marshes, Gibraltar Point is a dynamic place where wildlife flourishes. It was declared a nature reserve in 1952 and is now recognised both nationally and internationally as an area of outstanding wildlife and geomorphological importance.

What will you see?

The site supports a huge diversity of different plants and animals, ranging from plants that can survive daily soakings of salt-rich water, drying winds and scorching sun to grasses that build sand dunes.

Visit the reserve from late July to early September to see clusters of sea lavender carpeting the saltmarsh, turning it pink and providing a vital source of nectar and pollen for bumblebees and other insects. The mudflats around the Wash are a vital feeding ground for thousands of waders. Autumn at Gibraltar Point provides one of nature's most breathtaking spectacles as vast flocks of knots arrive from Canada and Greenland, swirling like clouds before an advancing tide.

Other highlights include the arrival of winter migrants, like brent geese, on the saltmarsh, and golden plover and lapwing, attracted by the grazing marshes and lagoons on Croftmarsh. They are joined by other arctic wading birds, including grey plover, dunlin, sanderling and bar-tailed godwit. Many will spend the winter on the Wash, while others rest and feed before continuing south.

September and early October see some of the highest tides of the year. These high tides advance slowly, covering the mudflats and saltmarsh as they approach. As the water slowly rises, huge flocks of wading birds are pushed off the feeding grounds. Tens of thousands of birds are forced into the air and the sight and sound of them passing overhead is breathtaking. The birds circle like huge plumes of smoke until they finally settle on higher ground. They pack densely on these areas of shingle and mud, waiting for the tide to fall.

Things you should know

- The visitor centre on site serves up delicious food.
- There is a network of paths and observation hides, and the full route around the reserve is about 3.5 miles.
- Wear wellingtons! Paths can get muddy and often flood at high tide, so waterproof footwear is essential.
- The 'Access for All' route is three miles long and suitable for wheelchairs and pushchairs.

PICTURED Knot at Gibraltar Point

'Tens of thousands of birds are forced into the air and the sight and sound of them passing overhead is breathtaking'

RESERVE NAME: Gibraltar Point
GRID REF: TF567580
NEAREST TOWN: Skegness
WILDLIFE TRUST: Lincolnshire Wildlife Trust
WEBSITE: www.lincstrust.org.uk
CONTACT: 01507 526667 / info@lincstrust.co.uk
OTHER RESERVES NEARBY: Snipe Dales Country Park (TF 330682)

109.
BUILD A SHELTER

If you're in a situation where you're forced to bunk down outdoors for the night, a shelter does three things: it protects you from the elements, shields you from unwelcome visitors, like biting insects, and provides psychological comfort. Hopefully you'll be building a shelter for the pure fun of it.

How to do it

1. Choose a spot close to a water supply and away from possible hazards – somewhere that's naturally sheltered is ideal. A canopy of trees will help to keep you warm and dry.
2. Construct a frame using thick tree branches pushed upright into the earth, angled so that rain will run off.
3. Stack and weave thinner, more flexible branches and twigs into the structure to provide more support and start closing the gaps. Make sure you leave an entrance hole.
4. Stuff leaves and other natural materials you can find into the grid-like structure, building up a layer of insulation that's at least 30 cm thick.
5. Find something to act as flooring or bedding – piles of dry leaves, pine needles or long grass. You don't want to rest directly on the ground otherwise you'll get very cold.
6. Crawl in and try it out.

110.
DISCOVER MAGICAL PLANTS

Numerous plants have healing properties and can be called upon to cure minor complaints. Most of us have reached for a dock leaf when we've brushed up against some nettles and would testify that their crushed leaves do help soothe a painful sting. There are plenty of useful herbs that you can grow at home or even find in the wild, but be very careful with what you use. It's worth taking a look at a herb guide for more detail on the health-giving properties of native plants. Never eat or drink a plant unless you are certain it is safe to do so and that any preparation you give it is safe and appropriate. Thoroughly research any recipes.

A few ordinary-sounding plants with magical properties

- **COMFREY** is known as 'knitbone' because it was once used in poultices to help heal fractures and breaks. It's also said to help soothe stomach ulcers and to be useful in the treatment of rheumatism and arthritis.
- **DANDELION LEAVES** are a potent diuretic and also a rich natural source of potassium. The root can be used to treat liver and gall bladder problems.
- **ELDER** is said to be good if you have a cold or flu, and has anti-catarrhal properties which make it useful for managing hay fever and sinusitis. It's also used to treat bruises and chillblains.
- **HOPS** have sedative qualities and can be used to relieve tension, restlessness, indigestion and nervous headaches.
- **STINGING NETTLES** have amazing health-giving properties as they are nutritionally very valuable. Make a soup from young nettle heads and it will help strengthen and support your whole body.
- **RIBWORT PLANTAIN** is a very common plant and is used to help calm bruises and wounds and speed up healing.
- **YARROW** is used to treat fevers and is thought to lower blood pressure, as well as working as a diuretic and urinary antiseptic.

111.
SPOT SNAKES

There are three snakes native to the UK: the adder, the grass snake and the smooth snake. Slow worms look like snakes, and often give the uninitiated a fright, but they're actually legless lizards. Reptiles can be found in heathland habitats, grasslands, meadows and semi-natural places such as railway embankments, road verges, golf courses, churchyards and even gardens.

Reptiles have bodies that are covered with scales or plates and shed their skin at least once a year. Snakes and lizards replace their teeth throughout their life. Cold-blooded, they source all their heat from the sun and so can often be found basking in its rays. They love sunny, south-facing slopes.

All British reptiles hibernate, overwintering in burrows or under logs protected from cold and predators. All snakes can eat their prey whole, as their jaws are surrounded by elastic skin and can open very wide, with the upper and lower jaws able to move independently.

Adders are found all over Britain and are our only poisonous snakes, though their bite is hardly ever fatal to humans. Adult adders reach lengths of about 65 cm. They're light grey or brown with black zigzag markings along the back. They enjoy a varied diet, feeding mainly on field voles but also mice, lizards, eggs and amphibians. Unlike other UK snakes, the adder gives birth to live young. Although they enjoy warm weather, during hot summers they will try to find cooler, damper areas.

Grass snakes are great swimmers and feed mainly on amphibians like toads, frogs, newts and small fish. Young grass snakes eat slugs. They can also climb and you could see one on a bush or hedge. They're long, growing to around 120 cm, and favour rough habitats with long grass. They like to lay their eggs in piles of warm, rotting vegetation. This is the snake you're most likely to see in your garden, although they become rarer the further north you travel and are hardly ever found in Scotland. They're dark green with black vertical bar and spot-shaped markings along their sides. They have a conspicuous gold collar marking too.

The rare smooth snake lives on heathlands in Dorset, Hampshire and Surrey, where it lays its eggs in sandy soils. They grow to around 70 cm and have distinctive round pupils in their eyes. They are grey, with

CLOCKWISE FROM TOP
Grass snake in a garden bush • Hatched grass snake eggs • Adder

two rows of darker brown or black markings along the back. Smooth snakes feed on other reptiles, mostly slow worms and lizards, but they can also be partial to pygmy shrews and young birds.

Reptiles are often needlessly killed. Many people are afraid of snakes, but snakes will usually avoid animals, including humans, that are larger than they are. Reptile populations have also suffered due to habitat loss and changes in land use. All native reptiles are protected by the Wildlife and Countryside Act and, for rarer species like the smooth snake, it's an offence to possess, handle, capture or disturb them.

112.
PLANT A HERB GARDEN

Freshly picked herbs transform a meal, spiking dishes with intense bursts of home-grown flavour. There are masses to choose from, they're low maintenance, happy in containers and can be grown all year round. Your herb garden can range in scale from a few pots on a window sill or doorstep, to a swathe of garden dedicated to all things culinary. Either way, the plants will be appreciated by wildlife as well as you.

Growing plants in containers is an easy way to green up hard surfaces. Most plastic and metal containers retain moisture better than clay ones but they're often less attractive or not as sustainably produced. Why not be creative and consider using old tyres, sinks, cans, buckets, a shoe or a teapot – anything that holds soil and water but allows excess water to drain?

Choose containers that are the right size for your plants. Pots that are too small will restrict root growth and you'll need to repot before the plant becomes established. Keep your containers close together. This allows the plants to shelter each other and increases the cooling effect of their leaves. Try to connect your containers to other green spaces to help wildlife move around.

A few easy herbs to try

- **BASIL:** A summer herb, basil is as delicious raw in salads as it is cooked in sauces. It's perfect with tomatoes and mozzarella. It's also rather nice with strawberries. Try growing it from seed or nurturing a small, shop-bought plant. Basil is not hardy.
- **BAY:** A rather ornamental-looking evergreen tree with leaves that can be used to infuse soups, stews and hot pots – anything that bubbles away slowly. Buy a small tree and keep it in a decent-sized pot so it can slowly grow tall and strong. A mature bay can survive outside in a sheltered spot in most winters.
- **CHERVIL:** A strong-tasting leaf with delicate filigree leaves that are great raw in salad. Fast growing, it's a cut-and-come-again crop that's easy to grow from seed.

'Freshly picked herbs transform a meal, spiking dishes with intense bursts of home-grown flavour'

- **CORIANDER:** Fast growing from seed and statuesque, coriander has pretty leaves that taste especially good in curries and soups. They're also great in a green salad. Allow the tiny sparkling white flowers to go to seed, dry them and then use them crushed in cooking.
- **LAVENDER:** A shrubby, drought-resistant evergreen, lavender has silvery leaves and sweet-smelling flowers that bees and moths love. Goldfinches love its seed heads too. Allow the flowers to dry on the bush. Collect the dried flowers and sew them into small cotton bags to keep your sock drawer smelling sweet. Buy a small plant and give it room to grow large and bushy.
- **MINT:** Cool mint leaves taste great mixed into natural yoghurt or crushed into a cocktail. Hard to grow from seed, try and get a cutting from a friend with a mint plant you like the taste of. They're thirsty plants and die back over winter. Mint can be very invasive so grow it in a pot.
- **OREGANO:** With small oval leaves ranging from green to a deep reddy purple, oregano creeps slowly at ground level but provides the grower with delicious leaves throughout the year.
- **PARSLEY:** Fast growing and tough, parsley has an almost bitter but fresh taste which is great in summer salads or sprinkled on top of a piping hot stew. It's hardy and will survive outside, even when conditions are freezing cold.
- **ROCKET:** A fast-growing, peppery leaf that tastes wonderful in green salads, or thrown in great piles on top of pizza or pasta. Rocket is really easy to grow from seed.
- **ROSEMARY:** A woody, evergreen bush that has pretty purple flowers and leaves that taste wonderful when roasted with garlic and potatoes or used to flavour oil. Another tough herb, the shrub will keep you supplied throughout the year. Buy a small plant and keep it in a decent-sized pot – it will grow large and bushy.

113.
HAVE AN ISLAND ADVENTURE
Looe, Cornwall

St George's Island is a unique reserve, as even getting to the island is an adventure in itself! En route visitors will have the chance to spot some of the marine and coastal life that make the island their home, with grey seals, cormorants and oystercatchers just some of the species that live in and around the reserve.

What will you see?

The island was kindly bequeathed to the Cornwall Wildlife Trust in 2004, and since then much work has been done to try to bring the island's many habitats to their full potential. By clearing some of the scrub and by grazing Hebridean sheep, the Trust aims to develop a grassland structure that benefits birds, invertebrates and a varied flora. Flowers and fine grasses associated with maritime grassland, such as thrift, sea campion and buck's-horn plantain, are some of the main candidates set to benefit and increase over the next few years.

Across the island small wild-flower meadows are also being created. These areas, combined with the mix of grassland, scrub and woods, have allowed numerous moths and butterflies to flourish. Most frequently spotted are speckled wood, meadow brown and red admiral butterflies, silver-washed fritillaries or the day-flying hummingbird hawk-moth. Visit in the summer to appreciate the full impact of an island in bloom and to witness the breeding seabird colonies at their raucous height.

There is a marked trail around the island that takes in the site of a Benedictine chapel, built in 1139 at the highest point of 150 m.

Things you should know

- Trips to the island are weather and tide dependent. Trips usually start at Easter and continue until September.
- Dogs are not allowed to visit the island.
- The path around the island can be comfortably walked in approximately 30 minutes.

St Georges Island from
near Hannafore Point

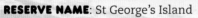

RESERVE NAME: St George's Island
GRID REF: SX258519
NEAREST TOWN: East Looe
WILDLIFE TRUST: Cornwall Wildlife Trust
WEBSITE: www.cornwallwildlifetrust.org.uk
CONTACT: 01872 273939 / email via the website
TRANSPORT: Take The Islander boat from the lifeboat station
slipway in East Looe. The crossing takes approximately 20
minutes and you have around two hours to explore the island

114.
WATCH SALMON JUMP
AT GILFACH FARM

Radnorshire, Wales

Gilfach Reserve is a traditional Radnorshire hill farm that has remained unimproved since the 1960s. Since 1988, the Trust has restored all the ancient field boundaries and fenced off the woodlands.

What will you see?

The meadows contain a range of ancient grassland species, including dyer's greenweed, moonwort, adder's-tongue fern, mountain pansy, parsley fern, heath dog-violet and eyebright. A large number of wax-cap fungi are also found across the reserve.

There are 55 breeding species of bird on the farm, including: dippers, grey wagtails, common sandpipers, pied flycatchers, redstarts, wood warblers, tree pipits, whinchats, stonechats, linnets, yellowhammers, siskins, redpolls, marsh and willow tits, stock doves, wheatear, bull-finches, buzzards, kestrels, barn owls, spotted flycatchers, meadow pipits and skylarks.

Insects abound too. Along the river damselflies, such as the beautiful demoiselle and emerald, can be seen, while common green grasshoppers and bloody-nosed beetles are frequently found in the grasslands. Butterflies include ringlets, wall browns, small heaths, green hairstreaks, and small pearl-bordered fritillaries. Larger mammals on the reserve include otters, polecats, stoats, weasels, badgers, foxes, hares and hedgehogs, while the railway tunnel is home to hibernating bats, including daubentons, natterers and brown long-eared bats.

It's best to visit in late autumn, when one of the reserve's most spectacular events takes place in the fast-flowing waters of the site's river. On their way to their breeding shallows, salmon make their annual migration upstream with furious effort and often in many numbers. Time your visit for one of the Trust's five salmon-watching days, held in November, for the best chance to see these athletes of the animal world. Those who are not able to attend one of the days can still look out for the salmon at their leisure, as the reserve's nature trail passes the Marteg Falls up which all the salmon must leap. The waterfall itself is a splendid sight at any time of year, but if you are lucky enough to spot otters chasing the salmon in the autumn, it is a wildlife spectacle you'll find hard to beat.

You should know

- The salmon-watching days get booked up months in advance, so make sure you get in early.

RESERVE NAME: Gilfach Farm
GRID REF: SN966716
NEAREST TOWN: Rhayader
WILDLIFE TRUST: Radnorshire Wildlife Trust
WEBSITE: www.rwtwales.org
CONTACT: 01597 823298 / info@rwtwales.org
TRANSPORT: Follow the A470 between Rhayader and Llangurig

WINTER

Winter can be bleak, no doubt about it, but it can also be stunningly beautiful. The sharp air seems cleaner somehow and one feels truly alive when the air is biting. Free of foliage, skies are huge and empty and it's far easier to spot wildlife that is still up and about. On frosty mornings, landscapes glitter and the ground's deliciously crunchy underfoot. Winter is an excuse to wear thick socks and ridiculous hats and to warm up after bracing walks with hot chocolate and buttered crumpets. It's a wonderful time to make plans for your garden, to help winter wildlife and to indulge in some serious armchair bird watching after baking a bird cake.

The frozen months can be especially tough for wildlife. Days are short and for many creatures, especially small birds, finding enough food to survive takes up almost every hour of daylight. The winter solstice on 21 December marks the shortest day. After this the days do get longer, though the coldest winter weather and highest chance of snow is often in January and February.

Winter wildlife watching opportunities are many, however. Trees have lost their leaves and it's possible to see the shape of their trunks and branches in vivid detail and to spot wildlife sheltering in them more clearly. Winter is great for bird watching, as long as you wrap up warm. Large numbers of migratory ducks, geese and swans are around, and other winter visitors to look for include redwing, fieldfare and sometimes waxwing.

Huge numbers of migratory species arrive and drakes are sporting their brightest and best plumage. Look out for flocks of migratory geese, especially in coastal areas, and for some of our less common ducks, including the pintail, goldeneye and long-tailed species, red-breasted merganser and goosander. Listen for tawny owls hooting, as they both begin their courtship displays in winter. Tawny owls are at their noisiest from December onwards.

»

'On frosty mornings, landscapes glitter and the ground's deliciously crunchy underfoot'

In winter many birds roost together for safety and warmth. Starling roosts can be spectacular, with huge flocks twisting and turning in the air at sunset before diving into cover and roosting for the night. In some places rooks, jackdaws, carrion crows and even ravens gather at communal roosts. Redwings and fieldfares will roost together in their thousands, often in young conifer woodland.

Some nature reserves, especially on the coast and on wetlands and heathlands, boast raptor roosts where you can spot hen harriers, marsh harriers, merlins and other birds of prey flying in to night-time roosts. The best time to track down bird roosts is from one hour before sunset, when you will see birds all flying in the same direction, heading to safe roost sites. Pied wagtails and even wrens gather in numbers to roost together for warmth.

If we get a festive frosting of snow it makes tracking wildlife far easier. Look for the double slot tracks of deer, or the prints of fox, badger or otter. Winter, even without snow, is the best time to find both tracks and trails because there are fewer plants to obscure marks on the ground and plenty of muddy areas and damp soft ground.

In your garden, winter is when you can most help wildlife, particularly birds. In the coldest weather fat balls are a great source of food, while sunflower seeds will ensure your garden is popular with greenfinches and chaffinches, as well as blue tits, great tits and perhaps coal and marsh tits. Winter is the best time to install bird boxes in your garden and also a great time to plant a tree or a hedge, as long as the ground isn't frozen.

Things to do in winter

- Plant a broad-leaved tree
- Make a wreath
- Feed the birds
- Plant a mixed hedgerow
- Make a nest box
- Swap seeds
- Witness a starling swarm
- Build a snowman
- Go on a long, bracing walk
- Make soup

115.
WITNESS A STARLING SWARM

Witnessing tens of thousands of starlings swirl and swoop through a winter sky is spectacular. Flocks of tightly packed birds form a seething dark cloud that stretches and contracts, reeling through the air as one pulsating, feathered mass. The evocative term for this is a 'murmuration'. Each bird performs fantastic aerial manoeuvres to confuse and avoid the birds of prey that are wont to attack. It's an amazing feat of animal organisation and coordination and absolutely not to be missed.

Recent research by Starlings in Flight, a pan-European group of researchers, has revealed that each starling focuses on seven neighbouring birds and responds to their wheeling movements, meaning the birds will always move back together if they are drawn apart. Previously it was thought that each bird only focused on the bird directly in front of it.

You're most likely to see a starling swarm on a fine, cold winter evening, just before dusk. They form as the birds head to a roosting place for the night. Keep an eye out from November until early March.

Where to witness a swarm

- Brighton Pier, Sussex (above)
- Hen Reed Beds, Suffolk
- Marsworth and Startops End Reservoirs, Hertfordshire
- Slimbridge, Gloucestershire
- Somerset Levels and Westhay Moor, Somerset

Water buffalo

116.
VISIT TEIFI MARSHES NATURE RESERVE

Cardigan, Ceredigion, Wales

Teifi Marshes Nature Reserve is one of the best places to see otters in Wales, and with a vistor centre, disabled parking, viewpoints and a children's play area it's well worth a visit at any time of the year. The reserve supports a number of different habitats, from pasture, woodland and hedgerows to freshwater marsh, reed beds and tidal mudbanks, and is home to a wide range of wildlife.

What will you see?

In spring and summer the reserve is alive with resident and migrant breeding birds, like reed bunting and sedge and cetti's warblers, as well as whitethroat, shelduck and moorhen. Numerous species of dragonfly and damselfly can also be seen during summer, including the emperor dragonfly, southern hawker and the scarce blue-tailed damselfly.

> *'To help manage the wetland habitats for wildlife a small herd of water buffalo are used to graze the marsh'*

In winter the area attracts large numbers of wildfowl, notably teal, wigeon and mallard. Water rail, snipe and curlew are also present in high numbers and can be easily seen from several bird hides and footpaths found throughout the reserve.

At this time of year you will also see the spectacle of thousands of starlings coming in to roost over the marsh. The best time to see them swarm is just before dusk on clear days throughout winter. To finish off your evening, take a short walk down to the viewpoint overlooking the River Teifi and try to catch a glimpse of the secretive otter. Due to the variety of wetland habitats, the Teifi Marshes Nature Reserve is one of the best places in Wales to see otters. Visitors often report female otters and cubs playing in the numerous pools, marshes and on the River Teifi itself, and dusk is a good time to see them.

To help manage the wetland habitats for wildlife a small herd of water buffalo are used to graze the marsh throughout the spring and summer months. Unmistakable, the water buffalo are easy to spot.

You should know

- The visitor centre and café are open every day from Easter through to Christmas.

RESERVE NAME: Teifi Marshes Nature Reserve
GRID REF: SN184455
NEAREST TOWN: Cardigan
WILDLIFE TRUST: The Wildlife Trust of South and West Wales
WEBSITE: www.welshwildlife.org
CONTACT: 01239 621600 / info@welshwildlife.org
TRANSPORT: Buses 430 and 390 from Cardigan stop in Cilgerran village; car parking on site
OTHER RESERVES NEARBY: Cardigan Bay Marine Wildlife Centre (SN3895659867)

117.
SEARCH THE STRANDLINE

A retreating tide always leaves fresh bounty for the eagle-eyed beach-comber. Get sand under your fingernails and savour the taste of salt on the tip of your tongue as you delve through the flotsam and jetsam along the strandline searching for signs of marine wildlife. Different beaches will reveal different treasures and what you find washed ashore will depend on the type of marine habitats beneath the waves further out to sea. A strandline is a line of clues, letting you play marine nature detective.

Things to look out for

CUTTLEFISH BONES – like polished mini-surfboards, these white oblongs are the internal shell of a cuttlefish, which acts like a built-in buoyancy aid.

CRAB SHELLS – look for moulted crab shells including the pink pie-shaped shell of the edible crab and the spiny shell of the spider crab.

SHELLS – almost any shore will contain a mix of shells. Look for familiar limpets, tiny periwinkles and shiny topshells. Peep inside to see if a hermit crab has taken up residence in an empty shell.

RAY EGG CASES ('MERMAID'S PURSES') – small black parcels with four long corners like stiff tassels. These once held the eggs of rays like the thornback ray. The yellowish cases with long, curly tendrils are from small sharks like the dogfish.

SPONGE – broken bits of natural sponge get washed ashore. Look for the pores in the sponge's body, through which it filtered water to extract the edible particles.

DRIFTWOOD – wood takes on a new lease of life when it's been polished by a thousand tides. Look for smooth holes bored by creatures such as the shipworm and gribble. If there's enough you could make a mini sculpture in the sand.

SEA WASHBALLS – balls of creamy-coloured capsules, which are the empty egg cases of the common whelk. Once used by sailors to scrub the decks of ships.

SHORE BIRDS – birds such as gulls, rock pipits and turnstones may be seen picking their way through the strandline in search of tasty morsels.

SEAWEED – there are lots of different kinds of seaweed. Look out for bladderwrack with its pairs of gas-filled bubbles that float the fronds when they're submerged, or big fat fronds of kelp and their knobbly holdfasts that attach them to rocks.

SANDHOPPERS – as you dislodge seaweed and sand you may see some flea-like creatures leaping into the air like popping corn. These are sandhoppers, small crustaceans that help clean up the beach by eating the rotting seaweed.

LITTER – sadly you are likely to encounter litter in the strandline too. Be careful and don't touch anything that looks unsafe.

Peacock butterfly

118.
MAKE ROOM FOR YOUR OWN VERY HUNGRY CATERPILLARS

Butterflies are in decline across the countryside, but they can easily be encouraged. Try allowing a patch of nettles to grow in a corner of your garden for butterflies to lay eggs on to witness the life cycle of these remarkable creatures.

The peacock butterfly with its distinctive markings was the first butterfly that I learnt to identify as a child. Our family always left a patch of nettles to grow beneath the lilac tree at the bottom of our garden, and whilst this meant that it wasn't much fun trying to retrieve lost balls from the middle of the nettle patch, it did mean that we always had lots of butterflies in our urban garden. Watching butterfly eggs hatch and the caterpillars munch their way through the nettles, before metamorphosing into their adult form is fascinating for adults and children alike. The life cycle story of the butterfly's metamorphosis was captured in Eric Carle's story *The Very Hungry Caterpillar*, a perennial favourite of young children everywhere. Cultivating a wild patch in your own garden will show your children that these caterpillars actually prefer to eat nettles rather than Swiss cheese and cupcakes.

While the peacock butterfly is not currently under threat, many other butterfly species are. Keep an eye out in your own nettle patch for other minibeasts as nettles can attract a range of wildlife.

Ellie Powers, Ecologist, joint winner of the Veolia Environnement Wild Things to Do competition

119.
BAKE A BIRD CAKE

In the winter months it can be hard for birds to find enough food to survive, so treat the birds in your garden by baking them a cake that will keep them nice and full up!

You will need ...

- Bird seed
- Cooked rice
- Grated cheese
- Dried fruit
- Breadcrumbs
- Chopped nuts
- Hard cooking fat (lard/dripping)
- A pine cone, coconut shell or yoghurt pot
- String

How to do it

1. Mix all the dry ingredients together in a bowl.
2. Add the fat and give it a good mix around.
3. Choose your feeder: you could plaster the mixture all over a fir cone, put it inside a coconut shell, or press it into an empty yoghurt pot.
4. Attach a string to your feeder before you fill it with the bird cake, ready for hanging.
5. Hang your feeder where you can watch birds without disturbing them.

120.
VISIT THE KNAPP & PAPERMILL
Alfrick, Worcestershire

This beautiful 27-hectare Knapp and Papermill reserve encompasses a range of wildlife habitats including ancient woodland, orchards and orchid-strewn meadows. Meandering trails and paths criss-cross the reserve making it an excellent place to while away a day watching wildlife.

What will you see?

Passing the visitors' information centre the path descends into the reserve brining you into the orchard. Look for Bramley and Queen Elizabeth apples growing in summer and autumn, and for nuthatches and woodpeckers probing the flaky bark on the old trees for a fix of insects. The orchard is also home to the rare and magnificent noble chafer beetle, declining across the UK and reliant on havens like this for survival.

After the orchard you can follow a circular trail along the Leigh Brook. Its dancing waters are a good place to spot the azure flash of hunting kingfisher, as well as other riverside wildlife including grey wagtail, dippers and many species of dragon and damselfly that patrol the waters in summer including the beautiful and banded damoiselles. Otters also live here although you will be very lucky to see one as they are mostly nocturnal.

RESERVE NAME: The Knapp & Papermill
GRID REF: SO751522
NEAREST TOWN: Great Malvern
WILDLIFE TRUST: Worcestershire Wildlife Trust
WEBSITE: www.worcswildlifetrust.co.uk
CONTACT: enquiries@orcestershirewildlifetrust.org /
01905 754919
TRANSPORT: Great Malvern and Worcester railway stations;
the reserve is at Alfrick Pound, approximately four miles from
the A4103

CLOCKWISE FROM TOP LEFT
Redpoll • Green Winged Orchid • Knapp Orchard

Carry on through to 'Big Meadow', where you'll need to keep a look-out for green winged orchids and in summer you may be greeted by clouds of meadow brown butterflies. A visit in summer will also take in several species of bee and other wildflowers and orchids.

Finally you'll walk through the woodlands to your right, home to trees such as wild service, small and large-leaved lime and some venerable oaks. In autumn look for nibbled hazelnuts bearing the distinctive toothmarks of dormice. The Trust manages the woodlands by coppicing which allows carpets of bluebells to emerge in spring, as well as other woodland flowers throughout the year. It also ensures a constant supply of habitats for many species of bird, including pied flycatchers and marsh tits.

Things you should know

- There is a steep hill leading down to the reserve and a number of stiles throughout.
- Information is available from a small information centre by the warden's house.
- Make a day of it with an eight-mile circular walk around reserves nearby.

121.
BUILD A DRYSTONE WALL

Drystone walls are so-called because no cement, or any other kind of mortar, is used to hold them together. Instead the wall is held up by the interlocking of the stones. Building one requires patience and skill, but they have many advantages, including the fact that they're great for wildlife, providing homes and shelter for reptiles, invertebrates, birds and small mammals. They're superb for lichen and mosses, too.

The traditional methods of construction used to build stone walls makes them very strong – many that you see in the UK are over two hundred years old, with lots built between 1750 and 1850. They're low-maintenance boundaries, requiring no nutrients from the soil and none of the upkeep that could be demanded by a hedge or fence. Ancient, they are like historical monuments and require a little respect. You shouldn't climb over stone walls, but instead use the stiles that are provided. Nor should you move the stones – if the top ones are removed from a stone wall, water and frost will destroy it.

Different regions have their own methods of construction, determined by the quantity and type of stones available. Boulder walls are a type of single wall made mainly of large flat boulder stones, around which smaller stones are placed. The largest stones are placed at the bottom and the wall tapers towards the top.

Another variation is a stone-clad earth bank, topped with scrub or turf. Here, as with many stone walls, the height is the same as the width of the base, and the top is half the width of the base. The double wall, meanwhile, is a structure made from two rows of large flattish stones rather than just one. Large through-stones are used at intervals, which span both rows and bind them together. A final layer of cap stones also binds both rows of stones together, topping the wall off neatly and preventing it from breaking apart.

If you're keen to give it a go, there are plenty of special drystone walling events and training courses you can enrol on across the UK. For example, Avon, Gwent and Gloucestershire Wildlife Trusts run walling sessions, or you could consider pursuing a master craftsman graded certificate from the Dry Stone Walling Association.

Drystone wall hot spots

- Cumbria
- Derbyshire
- Northumberland
- The Cotswolds
- The Peak District
- The Yorkshire Dales
- Many places in Ireland, Scotland and Wales

122.
SWAP SEEDS

Instead of sourcing all your seeds from a garden centre or catalogue, seek out a local seed swap. They take place all over the UK and tend to happen in February. You could pick up some interesting heritage varieties that aren't available in shops very cheaply or even free of charge. A seed swap is a sort of community fair, where growers exchange seeds from plants they've grown themselves. Often experienced local growers are on hand to offer useful advice, invaluable if you're a novice gardener.

Not only a way to get hold of a stash of new seeds to plant, seed swaps are also a great way to recycle any you have at home that you know you won't use. Pour half of that huge packet you have into an envelope or take along the freebies you've acquired from various magazines. One of the nicest things about seed swaps though is picking up home-grown seeds that have been collected from local people's plants.

Let your own plants go to seed so you have a supply ready to swap and plant next year. Allow seeds to ripen fully before you collect them ➤➤

and then harvest from your healthiest plants. To ensure seeds are ripe, wait until just before they would be dispersed naturally. The seed pod will become dry and will often change colour, probably from green to brown or white. The seeds inside will also change from green or white to brown or black. Dry the seeds thoroughly and then store them separately in airtight containers. Remember to label the seeds you collect and to keep them in a cool, dark place away from damp.

123.
VISIT HIGHGATE COMMON
Wombourne, Staffordshire

A gently rolling landscape, Highgate Common contains nationally-rare heathland, bare sandy stretches, open pools and tranquil woodland. A network of footpaths weave around the 95-hectare reserve.

What will you see?

Highgate Common supports a diverse spectrum of wildlife and was designated as a SSSI (Site of Special Scientific Interest) in 2006 because of its wide range of insects. The reserve is home to 130 species of bees, wasps and ants, 36 of which are nationally or regionally scarce.

One of the Common's most attractive residents is the tawny mining bee, a large, fluffy, ginger bee. Unlike the honey bee, it's a solitary bee, which means that rather than living socially in hives, it makes its own nest by tunnelling into the ground. In springtime, visitors will see scores of small holes and tiny volcano-like turrets in the sandy areas where the bee has made its home.

If you visit on a summer evening, you may be treated to a sparkly display of scores of tiny lights emitted by glow worms. And as well as insects, eagle-eyed walkers may also spot a range of reptiles basking in the sunshine during a visit. Slow worms, grass snakes and common lizards have all been recorded on Highgate Common.

In late summer, visitors to the Common can enjoy the breathtaking sight of a purple-heather carpet spreading across the heathland. Walkers may spot birds like stonechats, buzzards and skylarks swooping

Common lizard

overhead. Other floral highlights include delicate blue harebells and the cheerful yellow flowers of mouse-ear hawkweed.

Things you should know

- In August, Staffordshire Wildlife Trust holds a Bonkers about Bees fun day on the Common, with many bee-themed activities plus the opportunity to sample honey made by bees that drink nectar from the Highgate heather.
- A new community building with toilets recently opened on site, and there's an all-ability trail from the Pool car park that's suitable for pushchairs and wheelchairs.
- Highgate Common is always open and has eight car parks.

RESERVE NAME: Highgate Common
GRID REF: SO837897
NEAREST TOWN: Wombourne
WILDLIFE TRUST: Staffordshire Wildlife Trust
WEBSITE: www.staffs-wildlife.org.uk
CONTACT: 01889 880100 / info@staffs-wildlife.org.uk
TRANSPORT: Car parking on site

124.
VISIT WOODS MILL

Henfield, West Sussex

Woods Mill is a 44-hectare mixture of wetland and woodland habitats, providing an opportunity to experience a wide range of wildlife at first hand all year round.

What will you see?

Highlights include the elusive nightingale (three to four pairs regularly breed on the reserve), dragonflies, including brown and southern hawkers, common and ruddy darters, black-tailed skimmers and even the rare scarce chaser, plus a wide range of water, woodland and meadow plants. Birds to look out for include kingfishers, woodpeckers, bullfinches, blackcaps, robins, willow warblers and chiffchaffs, to name a few. The lake, a major focus of the reserve, is home to moorhens and herons.

For young visitors there are two dipping ponds teeming with smooth and palmate newts, pond skaters and water boatmen, so children can dip nets to discover the array of aquatic life living below the water.

The meadow is a regular hunting ground for barn owls and kestrels and the woodland areas provide dazzling displays of spring flowers each year, including bluebells, wood anemones and common spotted-orchids. In midsummer look for butterflies such as white admirals.

Things you should know

- Visit during April or May to hear the nightingales sing. Special evenings are available (booking essential) to learn about this elusive bird, with a trip out on to the reserve to hear them sing as dusk falls.
- There's a bird hide on the reserve and a platform over the marsh area offering marvellous views of the lake.

RESERVE NAME: Woods Mill
GRID REF: TQ218138
NEAREST TOWN: Henfield
WILDLIFE TRUST: Sussex Wildlife Trust
WEBSITE: www.sussexwt.org.uk
CONTACT: 01273 492630 / email via the website
TRANSPORT: Hassocks and Shoreham-by-Sea railway stations; limited parking on site
OTHER RESERVES NEARBY: Amberley Wildbrooks (TQ030136), Ditchling Beacon (TQ332129) and Malling Down (TQ423112)

125.
VISIT LACKFORD LAKES
near Bury St Edmunds, Suffolk

Lackford Lakes provide the visitor with magically close encounters with nature, be that the turquoise flash of a kingfisher, the splendour of a fishing osprey or the pure charm of a brood of new ducklings. They lie beside the River Lark and have been created from old gravel pits. Facilities like a visitor centre with car park, a network of footpaths and plenty of bird hides make visiting a simple pleasure.

What will you see?

Covering over 100 hectares, this is a superb site for wildfowl in both winter and summer, attracting tufted ducks, teals, pochards, gadwalls, shovelers and goosanders, plus there's a large winter gull roost. The site is also one of the best places in Suffolk for spotting kingfishers. Kingfishers are seen all over the reserve but are most easily seen from midsummer onwards, when numbers increase as the year's juvenile birds start learning to fish in the pools.

Passing birds of prey include the majestic osprey, while buzzards and sparrowhawks can be seen regularly. In the summer months, hobbies can be seen in hot pursuit of sand martins, swallows and an array of dragonflies. Cormorants are often seen fishing at the sailing lake or roosting in the tall trees by the lakes. Almost any migrant bird can turn up – black terns are regulars in spring but species like the little egret are becoming more common. Waders, like green sandpipers, common sandpipers and dunlin, can be seen during migration.

This reclaimed site has been quickly colonised by plants. Gipsywort, figwort, common fleabane and purple loosestrife occur by the water's edge and common centaury, common stork's-bill and biting stonecrop appear in the drier areas. Encroaching willows need to be kept in check so that the open water, which hosts clouds of blue damselflies, is not lost. Otters have become frequent visitors here.

CLOCKWISE FROM TOP LEFT
Lackford Lakes • Sparrowhawk • Pochard

Things you should know

- Lackford Lakes' visitor centre is fully accessible and has a range of facilities, including an information desk, gift shop, viewing gallery, toilets and a free car park.
- The Trust runs education courses for both adults and children throughout the year.
- The reserve and hide network are open from dawn to dusk every day.
- The mile-long Kingfisher Trail is negotiable by wheelchair, with ramped access to five hides, while the Orchid Hide, reached by a firm 150 m path from the car park, offers easy access for all visitors.

RESERVE NAME: Lackford Lakes
GRID REF: TL 799706
NEAREST TOWN: Bury St Edmunds
WILDLIFE TRUST: Suffolk Wildlife Trust
WEBSITE: www.suffolkwildlifetrust.org
CONTACT: 01473 890089 / info@suffolkwildlifetrust.org
TRANSPORT: nearest station is Bury St Edmunds;
free parking on site
OTHER RESERVES NEARBY: Grove Farm (TL 943652) and
Micklemere (TL 937698)

126.
HABITATS: FARMLAND

Humans have been farming in the UK for thousands of years, producing crops and materials, and feeding livestock. During this time, wildlife has adapted and moved into the farmed landscape to make the most of the riches it offers from flower-filled field margins to dense, bushy hedgerows; reed-lined ponds to seed-filled stubbles.

As traditional methods of farming have declined, however, and today's intensive farming practices have expanded through the landscape, there has been a rapid decline in the wildlife that is dependent on, and supported by, our farmed environment. Hedgelaying, rotational and diverse cropping, leaving winter stubble and field margins, and seasonal grazing are just some of the farming methods that have become less common in recent years, despite having many benefits for wildlife, the environment and food production.

Farmers are massively important in helping to look after our countryside and wildlife. Managed sensitively, farmland can support a huge range of species including barn owls, skylarks, brown hares, stoats, poppies, cornflowers and bumblebees. And as our natural habitats become fragmented and surrounded by 'wildlife deserts', well-managed farmland can provide a vital link between sites, helping wildlife to move about freely. Only by working on a landscape scale to create a giant patchwork of natural spaces can we really create 'Living Landscapes'.

Vine House Farm in the Lincolnshire Fens works closely with The Wildlife Trusts and is a good example of a farm managed in an environmentally sensitive way. The farms grow bird seed and sell wildlife-friendly products for attracting wildlife into your garden, helping you to help wildlife too.

127.
MAKE A WREATH

A home-made Christmas wreath created from natural materials beats any plastic wreath you could buy.

You will need ...

- Some flexible stems that can be bent into a wreath shape, like willow or hazel
- Conifer clippings or clippings from another bushy evergreen
- A selection of colourful and festive-looking leaves and berries, plus pine cones, nuts, seed heads and anything else you can find
- Holly and ivy work brilliantly, of course
- Dark green string
- Garden wire

How to do it

1. Make a hoop with your stems – interweave two or three to make the hoop strong. Secure it with some string. If you can't find suitable stems, an old wire coat hanger bent into shape works too.

2. Cover the hoop completely by tying conifer clippings or other bushy foliage around it. Wind some ivy round it too. It will now look like a naked wreath.

3. Start binding luxurious bunches of berries, small pine cones and other decorative bits and bobs you can find on to the hoop, disguising the string as much as possible with leaves.

4. Fill in any gaps with berries or pine cones attached to wire and then pushed into the wreath.

5. Use wire and string to make a strong hook that can be used to tie the wreath on to your front door.

Always gather your material sustainably and remember to leave plenty of berries and ivy for wildlife.

Scarlet Tiger Moth

128.
VISIT WINNALL MOORS
Winchester, Hampshire

Winnall Moors is one of the best bits of the Itchen Valley, featuring traditional water meadows, fenland, reed beds and wet woodland with networks of streams, chalk springs and ditches. Its size (64 hectares) and complexity make it a stronghold for water voles and otters. Since 2008 the reserve has been undergoing a transformation to restore degraded habitats and improve paths and activities for visitors thanks to funding from the Heritage Lottery Fund. Only moments away from the bustle of Winchester, it is well-loved by the local community.

What will you see?

The river Itchen has distinctive plant life, such as water crowfoot and lesser water-parsnip. On its banks purple loosestrife, water mint, gypsywort and various sedges provide cover which is used in spring by nesting birds, like little grebes and mallards and, in winter, the secretive water rail.

'Coming here is my daily dose of sanity'
– Visitor to the reserve

Reed beds and open mixed fen in the southern end of the reserve are dominated by tall grasses interspersed with wildflowers. Reed and sedge warblers breed here in the spring in large numbers, while bright-yellow marsh marigolds provide a welcome burst of colour after the browns of winter. Toadpoles gather in a wiggly black soup on the shallow edges of the pond. Along the river spot trout and grayling rising to catch mayfly on the water's surface.

Later on in the summer look out for tiny toadlets on the paths as they leave the water and disperse across the reserve. Also look out for the scarlet tiger moth, a day-flying moth with eye-catching red under-wings. You can find them basking in the sun on the boardwalks or feeding on the heads of aromatic umbellifer plants.

Follow the circular route round the southern end of the reserve and wander under tall trees, through open reed beds and beside the river. Relax on one of the rustic oak benches and watch out for kingfishers flashing past.

Things you should know

- Join an organised mini-stream-dipping day to discover damselfly nymphs, otter signs, freshwater shrimps, riverflies and little fish. Fed from underground chalk springs, the water is a constant 12°C – very cold if you were to dip in a toe.
- The entire route is suitable for pushchairs and wheelchairs. The surfaced paths mean it is safe to leave your wellies at home.

RESERVE NAME: Winnall Moors
GRID REF: SU485297
NEAREST TOWN: Winchester, Hampshire
WILDLIFE TRUST: Hampshire and Isle of Wight Wildlife Trust
WEBSITE: www.hwt.org.uk
CONTACT: 01489 774400 / email via the website
TRANSPORT: Winchester railway and bus stations
OTHER RESERVES NEARBY: St Catherine's Hill (SU484276)

'Feast on the landscape with your eyes as you eat your lunch. Drink in the smells, tastes and sounds of the great outdoors'

129.
WALK ALL DAY

Put on your comfiest and most hard-wearing shoes, pack some sandwiches and a flask of tea, then pitch out. Walk for mile after endless mile, taking huge, great, long strides and swinging your arms. Daydream and reminisce.

Walk along rivers and streams, through valleys and holloways. Cover the length of a beach and get lost in sand dunes. Explore woodland and hedgerows. Climb a hill and watch a waterfall.

Stop at a picturesque point for windswept refreshment. Feast on the landscape with your eyes as you eat your lunch. Drink in the smells, tastes and sounds of the great outdoors as you sip your tea.

Continue on your quest. Walk until the sun starts to drop and the air gets cooler. Go home with the rosiest of cheeks and enjoy the best night's sleep you've ever had.

LEFT Helvellyn, the Lake District, Cumbria

130.
ADMIRE A WATERFALL
Talgarth, Powys

Pwll y Wrach Nature Reserve covers 8.5 hectares of wonderful ancient woodland, which slopes down to the banks of the River Enig, with a network of paths for you to explore. At the eastern end of the reserve the river plunges over a spectacular waterfall into a dark pool below, which gives the reserve its name and translates as 'witches' pool'. Could this be the site where, many years ago, suspected witches were dunked into the cold waters of the river?

What will you see?

It is a delight to visit at any time of year. In spring the trees are clothed in their fresh green leaves and are alive with the sounds of chiffchaffs, ➤➤

*'In the winter the waterfall roars
as dippers bob up and down in the
River Enig, searching for food'*

with a heady carpet of bluebells and wild garlic around their roots. In summer the delicate foliage and white flowers of sweet woodruff and the yellows of yellow archangel and cow wheat speckle the woodland floor. In the autumn the leaves of the spindle trees turn a vivid red and they reveal their bright orange seeds, and in the winter the waterfall roars as dippers bob up and down in the River Enig, searching for food.

Two special plants to look out for in the spring are the rare bird's-nest orchid and toothwort. They are both unusual in that they lack the green chlorophyll that most plants have for obtaining energy from the sun. Instead they get their energy directly from the roots of trees and shrubs and from decaying tree leaves and wood.

Walk along the path from the main car park into the heart of the reserve and look out across the dingle through the woodland canopy with the River Enig twisting its way below. There, stop to appreciate the woodland bird orchestra that will serenade you with its many songs. Listen out for chiffchaffs, mistle thrushes, wood warblers, greater spotted woodpeckers and pied flycatchers, to name but a few.

Things you should know

- Children should be supervised by an adult when playing near the river.
- An easy-access trail provides a level surfaced path with a handrail to the centre of the site.

RESERVE NAME: Pwll y Wrach Nature Reserve
GRID REF: SO162328
NEAREST TOWN: Talgarth, Powys
WILDLIFE TRUST: Brecknock Wildlife Trust
WEBSITE: www.brecknockwildlifetrust.org.uk
CONTACT: 01874 625708 /enquiries@brecknockwildlifetrust.org.uk
TRANSPORT: Abergavenny railway station; parking on site

Pwll y Wrach waterfall

Four spotted
chaser dragonfly

131.
VISIT HATCH MERE

Frodsham, Cheshire

Hatch Mere is a Site of Special Scientific Interest and a beautiful place to visit. It's part of the Meres and Mosses Ramsar sites of the north and north-west Midlands, which are internationally important areas of open water and peatland, formed from meltwater after the last ice age.

What will you see?

The open water of the mere is circled with reeds that lead into water-based woodland and then dry woodland. The boggy areas around the water's edge are peat-based, created from the build-up of dead vegetation over thousands of years.

The mere is not fed by fresh water from a river or spring, but topped up by naturally acidic rainfall that's gradually turned the water slightly acidic. Consequently, the mere is home to species that have specially adapted to the conditions.

On the edges of the water, look out for yellow water lilies and starwort, as well as common reed and lesser reed mace. There's grey willow and alder in the boggy woodland, as well as county-rare species, such as tussock and tufted sedge.

To the north of the mere, sandy ground has formed an area of dry heath and oak/birch woodland. Within this area a dense thicket of bog myrtle exists, another county rarity, together with cross-leaved heath and heather. On the west side of the mere is an area of peat, home to cotton grass and eight species of sphagnum, including the nationally scarce Sphagnum flexuosum.

Hatch Mere is an important breeding ground for many bird species, including the great crested grebe, reed bunting and willow warbler. At least 13 species of dragonfly and damselfly have been recorded, including the hairy dragonfly and the variable damselfly. Several local and rare fly species and a nationally notable caddis fly have been recorded, as well as three aquatic beetles and two interesting species of snail – the ramshorn and spire snails. Several species of butterfly occupy this site, including the green hairstreak, plus a small population of common lizards.

Things you should know

- Next to the Carriers Inn, there's a small sandy beach where you can enjoy spectacular views across the mere.
- There's a good circular walk from Hatch Mere, but it covers boggy ground, so you need appropriate footwear.

RESERVE NAME: Hatch Mere
GRID REF: SJ553722
NEAREST TOWN: Frodsham
WILDLIFE TRUST: Cheshire Wildlife Trust
WEBSITE: www.cheshirewildlifetrust.co.uk
CONTACT: 01948 820728 / info@cheshirewt.cix.co.uk
TRANSPORT: Park in the Forestry Commission car park opposite the Carriers Inn on the B5152
OTHER RESERVES NEARBY: Hunter's Wood (SJ554763) and Warburton's Wood (SJ555762)

132.
VISIT ATTENBOROUGH NATURE RESERVE

Nottingham, Nottinghamshire

With its mix of open water and islands, the Attenborough Nature Reserve is a haven for wildlife and an easily accessible escape from the hustle and bustle of city life.

What will you see?

There is always something new to see at Attenborough, whether it's the blue flash of a kingfisher along the banks of the River Trent or great crested grebes diving for fish in the many ponds and pits that make up this much-loved nature reserve.

The area is an important site for winter wildfowl and often holds a high proportion of the county's shovelers, great crested grebes and diving ducks. Bittern regularly overwinter in small numbers. Breeding birds include common terns, kingfishers and great crested grebes, and visitors can get fantastic views of these and other wildlife from the reserve's bird hides.

The reserve is also the premier site in Nottinghamshire for breeding reed warblers and of county importance for its flora, with over 300 species recorded, including many scarce wetland species and 14 different species of willow. In terms of invertebrates, a number of butterfly species have been recorded, including the brown argus (a rare

RESERVE NAME: Attenborough Nature Reserve
GRID REF FOR RESERVE: SK516340
NEAREST TOWN: Nottingham
WILDLIFE TRUST: Nottinghamshire Wildlife Trust
WEBSITE: www.nottinghamshirewildlife.org
CONTACT: 0115 958 8242 / info@nottswt.co.uk
TRANSPORT: Attenborough railway station; by car, via the A6005

Attenborough's eco-friendly visitor centre

butterfly in Nottinghamshire), plus 101 species of hoverfly and 142 species of moth.

The eco-friendly Attenborough Nature Centre is at the heart of all reserve activity. Inside, visitors can learn about the reserve's wildlife, use the special nature table or enjoy the interactive touch-screen games. The centre also hosts a wide range of family-friendly activities, from guided walks to kids' clubs and craft sessions.

Things you should know

- The Attenborough Nature Centre was opened by Sir David Attenborough.
- The centre is a great place to enjoy a drink or light meal while enjoying views of the reserve, and you can also pick up leaflets there to make your visit more enjoyable.
- Facilities are all on one level with good access for wheelchair users.
- Although the paths around the reserve are level and well surfaced, some can get muddy in wet weather.
- There is good parking available on site, which requires a small donation.

133.
FEED THE BIRDS

The easiest way to spot birds is to get them to come to you. Prepare a feast and watch them flock in. In the depths of winter, when the ground is frozen and bushes have already been stripped of berries, birds can struggle to survive. Pickings are seriously slim and the nuts, fat and fruit that you leave in your garden can save lives.

Get creative with an old plastic bottle and some string and you can make a bird feeder in a few minutes, while pretty much anything can become a bird table. However, you will need to fix it to a 120- to 150-cm pole that can't be scaled: the key is to make sure that any feeding stations are not easily accessible by predators like domestic cats. Generally, open spaces make better sites for bird tables as they allow birds to keep an eye out for predators while they eat.

Feeders can hang from trees or, if space is limited, there are bird feeders available that attach on to windows and ledges. Many birds are also very happy to eat directly off the ground, but avoid scattering food late in the day as it could attract rats.

Make sure you source food that is bird-friendly – not all nuts are suitable for birds. Scraps of fat, cheese, porridge oats and bruised fruit will all be welcome treats. Brace yourself for visits from grey squirrels as well as birds. Make sure the birds have access to clean fresh water all year round. A shallow dish is ideal.

You can feed the birds in your garden all year round, but late winter and early spring are the key times to keep your feeders well stocked because natural food stocks are low and busy birds need energy to find mates and lay eggs. Never suddenly stop feeding wild birds. If you have to, gradually reduce feeding over a number of weeks. The birds have learnt to rely upon you.

In winter, fallen fruit and berries are beloved by hungry birds. Trees like holly are a valuable source of berries for woodpigeons and thrushes, while spindle berries are important for robins. Consider planting a mixed hedgerow in your garden. Aim for a varied mix of foliage, fruit and flowers, and include evergreen and thorny plants for winter shelter. Try berry-rich species like hawthorn, buckthorn and dog rose, spindle and crab apple, bramble and honeysuckle.

'The easiest way to spot birds is to get them to come to you'

South Walney Nature Reserve

134.
WATCH DIVE-BOMBING SEAGULLS

Walney Island, Cumbria

South Walney Nature Reserve forms the southern tip of a shingle island lying at the end of the Furness Peninsula. It has many large lagoons created by the extraction of salt, sand and gravel during the 19th and 20th centuries. The land was farmed by the monks of Furness Abbey in medieval times.

What will you see?

Every spring, large numbers of lesser black-backed and herring gulls still return and begin to set up nest territories. Other breeding birds include eider ducks, greater black-backed gulls, shelducks, oystercatchers, mallards, moorhens and coots. Of the 250 bird species recorded, most are passage migrants on their way to or from breeding grounds. These include common species, like wheatears, redstarts, willow warblers and gold crests, as well as more unusual species, which may have been blown off their normal migration route. In winter large numbers

> *'During the spring and summer,
> visitors can watch dive-bombing sea
> gulls – quite a spectacle!'*

of waders and wildfowl feed and roost around the nature reserve, both on the gravel pools and the intertidal areas.

The highly unusual vegetated shingle habitat is home to yellow horned-poppies, sea campion and biting stonecrop, while small areas of dune grassland survive with pyramidal orchids, Portland spurge, restharrow and wild pansies. The old gravel workings have developed their own communities, with striking plants such as viper's bugloss, henbane and alkanet. Salt marsh occurs in Lighthouse Bay, with species such as thrift, glasswort and sea purslane.

During the spring and summer, visitors can watch dive-bombing sea gulls – quite a spectacle!

Things you should know

- Cumbria Wildlife Trust employs a full-time warden to monitor and protect the birds and other wildlife.
- There are lots of activities for children, including a brass-rubbing trail.
- There is easy access for disabled visitors, and there is also a motorised wheelchair available for hire.

RESERVE NAME: South Walney Nature Reserve
GRID REF: SD225620
NEAREST TOWN: Barrow-in-Furness
WILDLIFE TRUST: Cumbria Wildlife Trust
WEBSITE: www.cumbriawildlifetrust.org.uk
CONTACT: 01229 471066 / mail@cumbriawildlifetrust.org.uk
TRANSPORT: Buses run between Barrow-in-Furness and Biggar
OTHER RESERVES NEARBY: Foulney Island Nature Reserve (SD246640)

135.
HABITATS: UPLAND

Covering around a third of the UK's land surface, upland habitats form the bulk of our wildest, most scenic and possibly most romantic countryside. The setting for many atmospheric novels from *Wuthering Heights* to *The Hound of the Baskervilles*, uplands are the open habitats of mountains, moors, heaths, bogs and rough grasslands. Here you will see fast-flowing streams with waterfalls, lakes and man-made reservoirs. Most of our upland habitats are found in Scotland, Wales, Northern Ireland and northern England, though there are smaller areas of moorland in Cornwall and Devon.

Though they may seem wild, moorland habitats have been shaped by people. Originally, these areas were covered in scrub and woodland, but a long history of clearing, grazing and burning the vegetation has created the moorlands we see today. Only the mountain peaks, rock faces, scree slopes and bogs are truly wilderness.

Upland habitats include acid grassland and marsh, heathland and peat bog. Wildlife-rich flushes accompany flowing water; stands of bracken occur on fells and rocky outcrops support scarce plants and provide nesting sites for birds of prey. The wildlife associated with upland areas includes birds such as ravens, peregrine falcons, red grouse, golden plovers and wheatears, alongside mammals like red deer, pine martens, wildcats and mountain hares. Typical plants include bell heather, ling heather, cross-leaved heath, bilberry, purple moor-grass and rowan trees.

Threats to our upland habitats include deforestation and overgrazing, mineral and peat extraction, pollution, development and climate change. The Wildlife Trusts are working on a local level to look after upland habitats and prevent further damage to these compelling places.

Hanningfield is great
for birdwatching

136.
VISIT HANNINGFIELD
RESERVOIR NATURE RESERVE

Chelmsford, Essex

Hanningfield Reservoir Nature Reserve is a 40-hectare mixed woodland reserve managed by Essex Wildlife Trust on the south bank of
the 352-hectare reservoir owned by Essex and Suffolk Water. This Site
of Special Scientific Interest has nationally important populations of
wildfowl and is one of the top places in Essex to watch wetland and
woodland birds. A visitor centre, complete with bat roost, makes your
visit even better.

What will you see?

This is a reserve for all seasons. In spring visitors come from far and
wide to see swathes of bluebells in Well Wood and Hawks Wood. This
is the time to listen to the wonderful spring chorus and to look out for
the floating nests of great crested grebes. Point Hide gives excellent
views of the reservoir's island, an important nesting site.

In summer look out for grass snakes and lizards basking in the sun.
The sheltered glades are excellent for butterflies, such as ringlets, and
the ponds are great for dragonflies. Listen for chiffchaffs, blackcaps

and other warblers and for the high-pitched calls of young sparrow-hawks. Watch thousands of swifts, swallows and martins feeding over the water, chased by the occasional hobby.

In autumn crunch through falling leaves and take in the autumn colours. Look for fungi and giant puffballs. When the reservoir drops, large areas of mud are exposed, which attracts a good mix of wading birds, including common, wood, green and curlew sandpipers.

Finally, in winter, large numbers of geese and duck can be seen, including gadwalls, wigeons, golden eyes, smews and pochards. The reflections of the sky on the reservoir are particularly stunning on bright winter days.

Things you should know

- Marked trails lead through meadows, ancient coppices and secondary woodland, by ponds and reeds, to four bird hides on the reservoir and to a restaurant at the Fishing Lodge. Pick up a trail guide at the visitor centre.
- Wildlife Discovery Kits are available for hire for children, as are binoculars in case you have forgotten yours.
- There's also an orienteering course around the reserve which can be used by groups or individuals.
- There are toilets with disabled access and the first bird hide on the trail is wheelchair friendly.
- The visitor centre and nature reserve are open 9–5, seven days a week, except Christmas Day and Boxing Day.

RESERVE NAME: Hanningfield Reservoir Nature Reserve
GRID REF: TQ725971
NEAREST TOWN: Chelmsford, Essex
WILDLIFE TRUST: Essex Wildlife Trust
WEBSITE: www.essexwt.org.uk
CONTACT: 01268 711001 / admin@essexwt.org.uk
TRANSPORT: Wickford railway station, where buses 14, 15 and 15A run to the top of Crowsheath Lane; free parking on site
OTHER RESERVES NEARBY: Crowsheath Wood (TQ725965) and Thorndon Country Park (TQ605915)

137.
WATCH BEAVERS
IN THE WILD

Argyll, Scotland

Venturing into the native woodlands of Knapdale Forest on the west coast is to enter Scotland's very own rainforest. Swathed in both native Atlantic oak woodland and coniferous plantations, much of this landscape is draped with mosses, ferns and lichens which prosper in the mild, wet climate of the Argyll coast.

What will you see?

Steep, rocky ridges, or 'knaps', cloaked in woodland and separated by narrow, often flooded 'dales' create a landscape unique in Scotland, where fingers of land jut out into the sea at Loch Sween. The inland freshwater lochs support an excellent array of dragonflies and rare pondweeds.

Visit between May and July to experience the full glory of the woodland plants. Other sights to see include wild flowers and woodlands, coastal scenery, archaeology and an array of birds, mammals and other charismatic wildlife. As well as being one of the most important sites in Europe for otters, the area is now also famously the site of the Scottish Beaver Trial, a five-year partnership project to trial the reintroduction of the European beaver. This marks the UK's first-ever formal wild reintroduction of a native mammal species. Known as a 'keystone' species, the presence of beavers should bring a vast number of benefits to other native Scottish wildlife, as well as wetland and waterside habitats. By modifying their habitats through coppicing, feeding and, in some cases, damming, beavers create ponds and wetlands which attract other species, provide a food source to others and can even help improve water quality. Visitors can follow the Scottish Beaver Trial's Beaver Detective Trail – you will be most likely to see beaver signs, such as damming, tree logging and lodge building, but there is always a chance of glimpsing the elusive creatures themselves. By timing your visit in the early morning or early evening, you will have the best chance of spotting these intriguing animals in the wild.

Things you should know

- There is limited parking space around the reserve, so visitors are advised to use the car park at Loch Coille-bharr and explore the site on foot from there.
- The beavers at Knapdale Forest are the first ones to live in Scotland for over 400 years.

PICTURED European beaver at Knapdale

RESERVE NAME: Knapdale Forest
GRID REF: NR766884
NEAREST TOWN: Lochgilphead
WILDLIFE TRUST: Scottish Wildlife Trust
WEBSITE: www.swt.org.uk / www.scottishbeavers.org.uk
CONTACT: 0131 312 7765 / beavers@swt.org.uk
TRANSPORT: The reserve is located approximately three miles north-west of Lochgilphead at the north end of the Kintyre peninsula; public buses run from Lochgilphead to Tayvallich

138.
VISIT PORTRACK MARSH AND MAZE PARK

Stockton and Middlesbrough, Tees Valley

Portrack Marsh and Maze Park together form an urban oasis in the heart of Teesside. The River Tees flows through the middle of these two reserves, increasing the range of habitats and species present.

What will you see?

Walk along the river through Portrack Marsh and you'll see a range of wetland birds, including teal, gadwall, wigeon, tufted duck, pochard and coot. There's a very good chance you will see seals feeding in the now cleaner River Tees. These hungry creatures have learned that the Tees Barrage has become a barrier to fish moving upstream. You can often see several seals catching very large salmon. In autumn take a look at the fish ladder to see the salmon migrating upstream.

On the other side of the river is Maze Park, which is a mix of post-industrial grassland that's alive with insects in summer. It's an ideal spot to see several species of butterfly, including the grayling and dingy skipper – both relatively rare in the North East. If you see one flying, watch it until it lands on the path and, as it closes its wings, it seems to disappear before your eyes as the colour of the underwing matches the ground so well.

If you visit in June time the vegetation will be teeming with six-spot burnet moths, either freshly hatched or attached as pupa to various plants. You can sit and watch them emerge in front of your eyes.

RESERVE NAME: Portrack Marsh and Maze Park
GRID REF: NZ465194
NEAREST TOWN: Stockton / Middlesbrough
WILDLIFE TRUST: Tees Valley Wildlife Trust
WEBSITE: www.teeswildlife.org
CONTACT: 01287 636382 / info@teeswildlife.org
TRANSPORT: Thornaby railway station

Robin singing in hedge

139.
PLANT A MIXED HEDGEROW

A mixed hedgerow provides food, nesting places and shelter for lots of birds, mammals and insects. It will create cool, shady places in what might otherwise be a hot, exposed site.

Planning

Mix at least five different species throughout your hedge and include mostly native plants, as generally these provide the best habitat for the widest range of wildlife. Aim for varied foliage, fruits and flowers throughout the year. Evergreen and thorny plants will provide winter shelter and protection from predators.

Add trees if you have space for diversity, height and extra shade. Good medium-sized trees include holly, crab apple or rowan. Good larger trees include oak, ash, whitebeam or silver birch. Be warned though, as some trees, such as oak, will be too big for the average garden.

A good planting mix would be: 70% from a choice of hawthorn, blackthorn, buckthorn, privet, beech, hazel and dog rose; 25% from a choice of guelder rose, field maple, spindle, crab apple, holly and yew; and 5% from a choice of climbers, such as honeysuckle, blackberry, ivy, native clematis and dog rose. »

How many plants you buy is up to you: one plant per metre gives a reasonable hedgerow but five per metre provides greater variety and more rapid cover. You can plant in a single straight line or, for a thicker hedge, plant a staggered double line. For a more natural hedgerow, plant in an irregular pattern rather than in long blocks of individual plants. Head to your favourite garden centre and choose bare-rooted plants (i.e. not in a pot), which are inexpensive and generally establish well.

Planting

1. The best time to plant a hedgerow is on a mild day between November and March – never plant into frozen ground.

2. Mark the shape and length of your hedge with cane and string.

3. Dig a trench along the line at least 45 cm wide and 30 cm deep (or big enough for the roots to fit comfortably). Double the width if you're planting a double staggered row of plants.

4. Stack the soil alongside the trench.

5. Remove weeds to reduce competition for water and nutrients.

6. Loosen the sides and base of the trench to help roots to grow and to improve drainage.

7. Place your plants in the trench one by one. Add plenty of peat-free organic compost as you backfill with the spare soil around the roots.

8. Lightly firm the soil around the base of each plant until it is stable and level with the surrounding ground.

9. Keep the roots of waiting plants in a bucket of water or cover with moist soil. Don't leave the roots exposed or they'll dry out quickly.

10. Step back every now and then to check you are still following your planting line.

11. Water each plant so that the water reaches just beyond the depth and spread of the roots. Keep plants well watered for at least one year until they are established (preferably use rainwater collected in a water butt and don't overwater).

12. When your hedge is established you can add plugs of woodland edge species and native wild flowers. Make sure your plants come from reputable dealers and are not taken from the wild.

Weeding and pruning

- Remove weeds by hoe or by hand to reduce competition for water.

- Allow plants to establish for at least a year before pruning.

- Late winter is a good time to prune because fruit and berries will have been eaten and your plants will be dormant.

- Trim your hedge to keep it at the height and spread you want. Cut out diseased stems and dangerous branches and stop species such as beech, hawthorn and hazel from growing into trees (unless you want to include a tree or two).

- Don't trim your hedge all at once – ideally, divide it into thirds and trim one third every year. This provides some undisturbed areas for wildlife and encourages flowering.

140.
TAKE A BARK RUBBING

A tree's bark is often one of its most distinguishing features and it's usually possible to identify the species of a tree from just its bark alone, as each has its own characteristic pattern.

To take a bark rubbing all you need to do is to hold a sheet of paper against the trunk of a tree and gently rub the side of crayon over it. You can take rubbings of pretty much anything – leaves also work well. Collect fallen leaves and then take a rubbing while resting them on a flat surface.

A nice idea for home-made wrapping paper is to decorate plain brown parcel paper with bark rubbings done with a colourful crayon. You could even make a gift tag from a large dried leaf.

141.
EXPLORE A MOOR

Blacka Moor, Sheffield

Situated just within the Peak District National Park and on the suburbs of Sheffield, Blacka Moor is much loved for its feeling of wilderness and its changing character, from wind-swept heath to sheltered wooded valleys and sunny glades.

What will you see?

For those just starting out nature watching, there are many garden birds that have more adventurous cousins living on Blacka Moor. Look out for robins, great and blue tits and the surprisingly noisy wren in the bushes and trees of the woodlands, especially in Strawberry Lee Plantation. Sparrowhawks will be looking for the little birds too, so keep an eye out for them swooping into bushes, looking for a meal.

In the spring, the drystone walls around the plantation and along the track to the pastures are the best places to spot common lizards basking in the sun. The summer months are a good time to lounge around in the pastures and watch skylarks fly straight up into the air, warbling their song into the sky.

With a bit more practice, there's even more to discover. Red deer can be seen bashing horns and bellowing in October out on the open heath, or quietly grazing in groups on the heath and in the woodland at other times of year. To have a chance of watching the deer without startling them, you'll need to stay very quiet, move slowly and hide behind trees and bushes.

RESERVE NAME: Blacka Moor
GRID REF: SK296803
NEAREST TOWN: Sheffield
WILDLIFE TRUST: Sheffield Wildlife Trust
WEBSITE: www.wildsheffield.com
CONTACT: 0114 263 4335 / mail@wildsheffield.com
TRANSPORT: Parking available at Hathersage Road and Strawberry Lee Lane entrances; buses from Sheffield

LEFT TO RIGHT
Blacka Moor • Wood Warbler

Take a wet wander through Cowsick Bog in the summer to see the beautiful displays of yellow bog asphodel found to the side of the flagged path, and the wispy white heads of hare's-tail cotton grass.

For those with lots of experience of species-seeking, there are a few more elusive beasts to find, like the strangely named heath rustic and golden-rod brindle moths. While strolling through the woods, you may be lucky enough to see the elusive treecreeper or hear the wood warbler with its strange song that sounds like a spinning penny. Adders have been recorded in the past at Blacka Moor, but not for a while now; could you be the first to find one in a decade?

Things you should know

- Blacka Moor has a wide network of bridleways and footpaths, but most are not suitable for wheelchairs and pushchairs as they can be rough and muddy.
- The whole network can be walked in about four to five hours or a short walk (45 minutes) can take in woodland, heathland and the pastures.
- Dogs should be kept under close control or on a lead.
- The reserve is open all year round.

142.
MAKE A NEST BOX

Nest boxes provide safe homes for breeding birds and it's a joy to see a family grow up in your garden. A dwindling number of old, hollow trees means bird boxes are more important than ever. An estimated two million fledglings are raised in UK nest boxes each year, and one box alone could be home to more than 100 babies over a ten-year stretch. Making your own is a particularly satisfying project, not least because it is reletively simple to do!

The first thing to think about is what species of bird you want to use it, as this will determine how big the entrance hole needs to be. For small birds, a 2.5-cm diameter is best. Bigger birds, like great tits and sparrows, need a 3.2-cm hole, while robins and wrens favour open-fronted boxes.

You will need ...

- Rough-cut timber, untreated and at least 1.5 cm thick
- Some old rubber or a hinge
- 20-mm nails

- A saw
- A hammer
- A hand brace or drill
- A pencil, ruler and scissors

How to do it

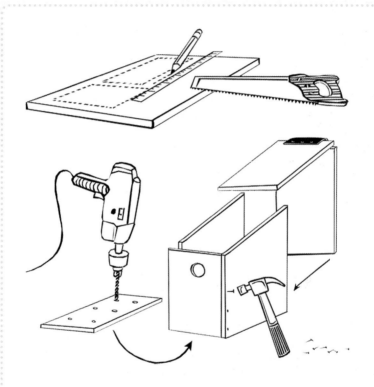

1. Mark out and saw panels, as shown in the diagram. Remember to include a couple of drainage holes to ensure any rain that gets in can drain out again.
2. Nail the panels together. Fix on the roof panel with a hinge or strip of old rubber.
3. Place the box 2–5 m above the ground, somewhere sheltered.

143.
VISIT COLLEGE LAKE
Tring, Buckinghamshire

Nestling at the foot of the Chiltern Hills, College Lake is one of the best places in Buckinghamshire to spot water birds dabbling in the shallows or swooping through a sunset-lit sky. Lapwings, redshanks, wigeons, common terns and oystercatchers are just some of the regular visitors. There are 11 bird hides overlooking the lake and marsh, offering a chance to catch a glimpse of rarer visitors too, like majestic ospreys and hobbies hunting dragonflies over the water.

What will you see?

In spring, hares engage in frenzied boxing matches and butterflies dance through the grassland on sunny days. In summer, the fields are a riot of colour as traditional cornfield flowers burst forth and bees buzz through the meadows. In autumn, the leaves turn golden in the hedgerows and the shiny red fruits of the guelder-rose offer a feast for tiny mammals fattening up for the cold ahead. And in winter the lake becomes a meeting point for all kinds of waterfowl, from colourful teals to monochrome tufted ducks.

'In spring, hares engage in frenzied boxing matches and butterflies dance through the grassland'

College Lake also has a rich history. A hundred million years ago it was at the bottom of a warm sea. Tiny algal plants settled on the sea floor, creating a chalk bed in which other sea creatures, like sharks, ammonites and urchins, became fossilised. More recently, a mere two hundred thousand years ago, the scene at College Lake was very different: it was a savannah with grassy plains filled with massive animals, such as mammoths, lions and bison.

In the 1960s, the chalk at College Lake was quarried by huge machinery. The quarrying finished in the 1990s but its legacy lives on: the huge pit left behind is now the lake and marsh that supports so much wildlife.

Hares boxing

During quarrying, fossils of the creatures that once inhabited the area were discovered in the chalk, including a huge mammoth tusk that now resides in a glass-covered fossil pit in the visitor centre.

You should know

- There's disabled access and a tramper vehicle available for free hire – contact the visitor centre.
- The eco-visitor centre has a cafe and great views.

RESERVE NAME: College Lake
GRID REF: SP934140
NEAREST TOWN: Tring
WILDLIFE TRUST: BBOWT
WEBSITE: www.bbowt.org.uk
CONTACT: 01442 826774 / collegelake@bbowt.org.uk
TRANSPORT: Tring railway st.; bus stop nearby; parking on site
OTHER RESERVES NEARBY: Dancersend Nature Reserve (SP904088), Aston Clinton Ragpits (SP887107) and Weston Turville Reservoir (SP859095)

Urban peregrine falcon

144.
SPOT URBAN RAPTORS

Peregrine falcons are swapping their traditional cliff-top homes for manmade urban ones, where the pickings are rich and the living is good. Persecuted and poisoned to the brink of extinction in the UK, the recovery of these handsome raptors has resulted in pairs returning to the very heart of our towns and cities.

Peregrines traditionally nest on high, remote cliff faces and mountain crags, but have learned to adapt to artificial sites – what could be better than a high-rise tower block or church spire with space to breed, ready-made plucking sites and a limitless supply of tasty rats and feral pigeons?

Another reason why urban areas are becoming top choices for home-making peregrines is the weather. In their natural ranges, pairs will often guard their nesting sites throughout harsh winter weather but be forced to migrate to coastal lowlands when food supplies get very low. With milder temperatures in towns, especially further south, peregrines can afford to stay on and protect their warm nesting territories all year round.

The peregrine falcon's vital statistics are impressive. It's the world's fastest moving bird, achieving speeds of up to 150 mph during spectacular 300-m swoops. Courtship involves dramatic aerial acrobatics, with loop-the-loops and the passing of food gifts mid flight.

Other raptors you could spot in urban areas include sparrowhawks, kestrels and common buzzards.

The best ways to protect these dashing birds of prey is to admire them from afar and keep records of when and where you see them. Up-to-date records are invaluable tools for conservationists monitoring species. Avoid using pesticides as well – it was DDT that nearly wiped out peregrines back in the 1960s.

Where to spot urban raptors

- Fort Dunlop, Birmingham
- Derby Cathedral, Derby
- Tate Modern, London
- Exchange Square, Manchester
- St Andrew's Spire, Worcester

145.
WATCH WILD HORSES

Dartmoor ponies

Small, fast and agile, Dartmoors are the native pony breed of Devon and they've been living on the county's wild upland moors since the Middle Ages. They're working ponies – they were used extensively by the tin-mining industry and later in the coal mines. Ponies even used to be bred at Dartmoor Prison to be used by guards when escorting prisoners. They're now considered to be an excellent riding pony for children. Numbers have declined and this breed is also classed as endangered, with the population estimated at around 5,000.

»

Exmoor ponies

Exmoor ponies

Brown, stocky and strong, the Exmoor (above) is Britain's oldest breed of native pony and the most similar to the first wild horses of Europe. Some still roam freely on moorland in Devon and Somerset. First domesticated by the Celts, the history of these herds is inextricably linked to man. There are only around 1,000 Exmoors worldwide and the breed is classed as endangered. The Exmoor herds that roam freely and breed in their natural habitat are unique but they're not totally wild – each one has a name, branding marks and an owner.

Conservation grazing

Conservation grazing is the use of livestock to manage conservation sites and to encourage the wildlife that the sites support. Grazing can create the right conditions for rare and fragile plants to grow and flourish. Groups of Exmoor and Dartmoor ponies are being called into ecological service around the UK, helping to maintain the natural balance of indigenous flora and fauna. Some Wildlife Trusts also use Konik ponies, descendants of the original wild horses of Europe.

146.
VISIT BRANDON MARSH NATURE RESERVE

Brandon Marsh Nature Reserve, Warwickshire

Nestled on the banks of the river Avon, Brandon Marsh is a 200-acre nature reserve. Formerly the site of a sand and gravel quarry, it has since been allowed to revert to a more wild and natural state. There are now several lakes and wetlands which provide havens for a variety of waterfowl, migratory or breeding birds and other wetland animals. The meandering nature trails and bird hides also provide the perfect opportunities to observe the wildlife and enjoy nature.

What will you see?

Brandon Marsh is particularly well-known for its birds, so it is the perfect place to do a bit of species spotting and get a few ticks on your annual list.

Depending on the time of your visit you could see migrating waders, breeding warblers, year-round residents like kingfishers, or rarities like bittern. With a range of habitats including reedbeds, open water, grassland and woodland, the site attracts a lot of wildlife, including many butterflies, moths, damselflies and dragonflies.

During your visit, make sure you keep your eyes peeled amongst the riverbanks and reedbeds for anything small, brown and furry. Warwickshire Wildlife Trust run a water mammal monitoring programme, and they want to hear from you if you've spotted otter, mink or water vole in the county, so make sure you note your sightings down!

RESERVE NAME: Brandon Marsh Nature Reserve
GRID REF: SP386761
NEAREST TOWN: Coventry
WILDLIFE TRUST: Warwickshire Wildlife Trust
WEBSITE: www.warwickshire-wildlife-trust.org.uk
CONTACT: 024 7630 8999
TRANSPORT: On-site parking

147. HABITATS:
PEATLAND, BOG AND FEN

Created over thousands of years, peat is a dark, fibrous material familiar to those of us who enjoy gardening. But this useful product has both a long history and an exciting range of wildlife associated with it today.

Plants that live in waterlogged conditions, such as richly coloured sphagnum mosses and pretty pink heathers, do not completely rot when they die because there is little oxygen available. Instead, along with the organic remains of fungi, trees and insects, they form peat. Due to this lack of decomposition, well-preserved artefacts, animals and even bodies have been found by archaeologists exploring peatland.

Bogs are one of the habitats of peatlands. Blanket bogs usually form in rainy, cold, upland areas, where the wind sweeps through your hair and tufts of white cotton grass brighten the dark landscape. Raised bogs develop naturally in lowland areas, such as river valleys, and have dome-shaped surfaces with hollows and pools. Bog plants include fly-eating round-leaved sundews, bright yellow bog asphodel and hare's tail cotton grass. Breeding birds include greenshank, golden plover and dunlin.

Fens also form on peatland. Many occur at the margins of lowland lakes and support rushes, sedges and grasses, along with wild flowers like meadowsweet, marsh helleborines, early marsh-orchids and forget-me-nots. Eventually, dead plant material builds up, cutting off the groundwater which feeds the fen and the building blocks of bogs – sphagnum mosses – begin to colonise.

Agriculture and forestry have damaged large areas of peatland, but today commercial peat extraction for horticulture is the major threat. The Wildlife Trusts encourage every gardener to do their bit by buying peat-free composts.

PICTURED Peatland, Lancashire

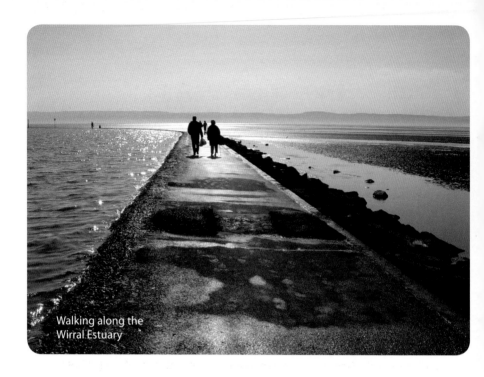

Walking along the Wirral Estuary

148.
WALK IN A DINOSAUR'S FOOTPRINT

Hilbre Island, Wirral

On the Wirral peninsula there is an abundance of wildlife and nature walks to choose from. Myself, my husband and our two young boys enjoy mud filled walks in our wellies along the many beaches and grassy trails that are scattered along the peninsula's coastline. One of our favourite walks is to Hilbre Island, where you can often spot seals as well as other spectacular wildlife.

Hilbre Island is the largest of a group of three islands at the mouth of the estuary of the River Dee, about a mile from Red Rocks, the nearest part of the mainland of the Wirral peninsula.

If you had stood on the island in the Triassic era, 240 million years ago, you would have been in the equivalent of the Sahara Desert. At that time, what is now Britain was on the equator, and you would have been in the middle of a massive expanse of sand, with huge dunes and muddy, vegetated water channels. Dinosaurs roamed, leaving their footprints in the mud. You can still see the footprints now fossilised in the sandstone. It is thought that the islands were part of the mainland until the end of the last ice age, about 10,000 years ago. The increased water levels caused by the melting ice cut a channel between West Kirby and what became the three islands.

My sons and I love nothing more than squelching our way to the island, imagining which dinosaurs may have roamed here and trying to spot the animals in residence today.

Other places to walk with dinosaurs

- The Jurassic Coast, Dorset
- Compton Bay, Isle of Wight
- Beachy Head, East Sussex
- Herne Bay, Kent
- Lavernock Point, Glamorgan

Jeni Howard, Operations Supervisor, joint winner of the Veolia Environnement Wild Things to Do competition

149.
WALK BAREFOOT

Free your feet and feel the earth and the ocean between your toes.

Walk barefoot in and through and over ...

- Shallow seawater, with breaking waves tickling your toes
- Hot sand, with grains whipping your ankles
- Long grass, getting damp with dew
- Gentle streams, with bubbles massaging your soles
- Warm mud, letting clay ooze between your toes
- Smooth pebbles that have been beaten soft by the sea
- Glassy lochs, with fish nibbling at your shins
- Coastal rocks that are slick with seaweed

'Choose a native tree from a reputable supplier. Natives are more likely to benefit British wildlife.'

150.
PLANT A BROAD-LEAVED TREE

Broad-leaved trees provide food, shelter and nesting places for many species of wildlife. They give a garden structure and increase opportunities for wildlife to colonise. Trees also improve soil in the form of leaf mould and create cooling shade during hot summers. This can extend the range of plants that you can grow in your garden and attract wildlife that prefers shady conditions.

Think about the size of your garden, its aspect and soil type. Think about how high you want the tree to grow and how it might affect buildings, drains, walls, fences and lawns. Choose a native tree from a reputable supplier or garden centre. Natives are more likely to benefit British wildlife. Choose from bird cherry, crab apple, alder, birch, oak, hawthorn, holly, hazel, yew and silver birch. If you want non-native trees, choose species that give food and shelter to wildlife. Aim for variety if you have space for more than one tree.

The best time to plant bare-rooted and container-grown trees is from November through to March, but never plant when the soil is frozen. Smaller plants are cheaper than larger ones and establish faster. A 1-m bare root whip, which costs £1–2, will experience less stress (if planted properly) and within two years will have probably overtaken a 2-m container-grown tree that cost £50.

With bare-rooted trees, inspect the roots to ensure that they are moist and there are many fine root hairs. This indicates a healthy tree. Keep the roots moist and sheltered from the wind before planting. With container trees, don't buy one with roots growing out of the bottom of the container because they might be pot-bound. If the tree is in leaf, leaves should be fresh and healthy. If the tree is bare, check that the branches are not brittle. Stand in a bucket of water for one hour before planting to loosen the soil and roots.

PICTURED Oak tree

Tree Planting Tips

Digging the hole

1. Dig a hole a little deeper than the roots and at least three times wider than the diameter of the root ball or the spread of the roots.
2. Loosen the sides and bottom of the hole to help the roots establish.
3. Add about 5 cm of peat-free organic matter in the bottom of the hole.
4. Remove surrounding weeds and grass to reduce competition for water.

Planting bare-rooted trees

1. Build a mound of earth in the centre of the hole.
2. Use the mound to position the tree and splay the roots around it.
3. Gently backfill with soil, carefully filling the spaces around the roots.
4. Gently but firmly press the tree into position.
5. Water immediately with enough water to reach just beyond the spread and depth of the roots.

Planting container-grown trees

1. Slowly remove from the container, taking care not to damage the crown or stem.
2. Gently loosen the roots if they are compacted and place the root mass carefully into the hole.
3. Backfill with soil and position with gentle but firm force.
4. Water well.

Looking after your young tree

- Keep your sapling well watered for at least 18 months until it has established. Use rainwater collected in a butt and water during early morning or evening, as less water will evaporate than during the heat of the day. Adding a layer of organic matter around the trunk will retain moisture and suppress weeds. »

- Taller or rapidly growing trees may benefit from staking about a third of the way up the trunk. You should secure the stake with a flexible tree tie that allows the trunk to move a bit. Make sure the trunk does not outgrow its tie.

- Be careful not to damage your tree when you're using a strimmer. You can protect it with rabbit or deer guards if necessary.

151.
USE A TELESCOPE

If binoculars are simply not enough when it comes to satiating your bird-spotting desires, a telescope is worth consideration. Not as portable as a humble pair of bins, telescopes are best used when you've found a great viewing spot where you plan to spend some serious time watching for wings. Perhaps this spot will be in a bird hide or even in your garden if you've got good views at home.

Telescopes have powerful lenses, allowing you to zoom in on objects that are incredibly far away. Not only good for wildlife watching, they also reveal a whole new sparkling world of stars and galaxies if you point one skywards at night. Who knew the surface of the moon had such details?

As with all gadgets, telescope choice is somewhat endless. Do you pick straight or angled, fixed focus or zoom? They should all come with some kind of support, like a tripod. You can spend a lot of money if you wish. The best thing to do is to try a few out before buying anything. Have a go on fellow birdwatchers' scopes and ask for their opinions. Look at online discussion forums and customer reviews.

Telescope magnifications range from 15x all the way up to 60x. If a telescope has a fixed eyepiece, 20x or 30x is normal, but zoom eyepieces that can switch between 20x to 60x are also available. A compact 60-mm telescope with a wide angled 20x eyepiece is considered fine for general use, with larger scopes better suited for fixed-position bird watching.

152.
CYCLE ALONG THE COAST

Druridge Bay, Northumberland

The Northumberland Wildlife Trust manages five nature reserves along Druridge Bay. Most of these are set slightly back from the coast itself, behind the protective lines of sand dunes, and some owe their existence to coal mining.

What will you see?

At Cresswell Shore and Pond reserve, the shore's large wave-cut platform contains many shallow rock pools. Wildlife includes porcelain crab, butterfish, shanny, kelp and coral weed. Bird populations include turnstone, purple sandpiper, sanderling and ringed plover. The pond provides a valuable place for passage migrants. There are reed-beds around the margins and small areas of salt marsh with sea aster providing a splash of purple in late summer.

The Druridge Pools site is part of restored opencast coal workings and consists of a deep lake and wet fields. The lake supports large flocks of wintering wildfowl, including wigeon, teal and goldeneye. The wet fields are very good feeding sites, especially for birds such as snipe, redshank and teal.

Large numbers of waterbirds use the East Chevington ponds and their margins, including greylags and pink-footed geese. Skylarks, stonechats and grasshopper warblers breed on the site, as well as reed buntings, sedge and reed warblers. The grasslands contain dyer's greenweed, lesser butterfly and northern marsh orchids. Butterflies, such as the common blue and meadow brown, are seen regularly in summer. In 2009, marsh harriers bred at East Chevington for the first time in 130 years.

In the late spring and summer the Hauxley Reserve provides a colourful floral display, from the diminutive maiden pink to huge spiky teasels. Viper's bugloss, northern marsh orchid and common spotted orchids also grow here. In addition to wetland birds, Hauxley is also a good place for tree sparrows and an array of other woodland birds.

The sites are linked together by the Coast and Castles cycle route, and are also part of the North Sea Trail. Why not take a ride through the reserves as you go?

You should know

- All sites, apart from Cresswell Hide, have paths and hides, most of which are suitable for wheelchair access.

RESERVE NAME: Druridge Bay area (including the reserves of Cresswell Shore and Cresswell Pond, Druridge Pools, East Chevington and Hauxley)
GRID REF: Cresswell Shore and Cresswell Pond – NZ283944; Druridge Pools – NZ275963; East Chevington – NZ270990; and Hauxley – NU285023
NEAREST TOWN: Alnwick
WILDLIFE TRUST: Northumberland Wildlife Trust
WEBSITE: www.nwt.org.uk
CONTACT: 0191 284 6884 / mail@northwt.org.uk
TRANSPORT: Cresswell Shore and Pond and Druridge Bay are north of Cresswell village; East Chevington lies south of Druridge Bay Country Park (car parking on site); Hauxley is accessed off the road leading between High and Low Hauxley villages

INDEX

FLORA

ACKNOWLEDGEMENTS

Adam Cormack, Helen Babbs, Sara Bellis, Emma Bradshaw, Gianni Brancazio, Jo Clark, James Collins, Johanna Cormack, Anna Guthrie, Paul Hamilton, Lynn Hatzius, Clive Hebard, Kevin Hurst, Kate Inskip, Zoe Johnston, Amy Lewis, Natasha Liedl, Ellen Marshall, Mary Porter, John Plumer, Catherine Rees, Mark Searle, Helen Szirtes, Lynn Victor, Helen Walsh and everyone at The Wildlife Trusts.

Image credits

The photographs in this book are copyright of The Wildlife Trusts, iStock, northeastwildife.co.uk, Shutterstock and Alamy, or as noted:

p5 Red squirrel – Damian Waters/ drumimages.co.uk
p9 Rockpooling at wembury – Nigel Hicks
p10 Underwater shallows, St Abbs Head – Paul Naylor/marinephoto.co.uk
p23 Robin – Neil Aldridge/ neilaldridge.wordpress.com
p24 Osprey – Leicestershire & Rutland Wildlife Trust
p28 Pink-footed geese - Laurie Campbell/ lauriecampbellphotography.com Trust
p32 Painted lady – Keith Warmington/ warmies.co.uk
p36 Den building at Wessington – Herefordshire Nature Trust
p38 Basking shark in Manx waters – Eleanor Stone/Manx Wildlife Trust
p41 Silent Valley Nature reserve – Jane Corey/Gwent Wildlife Trust
p44 Blackbird – Robography /Alamy
p55 Mannesz Pond – Alderney Wildlife Trust
p60 Puffin – Damian Waters/ drumimages.co.uk
p73 Dragonfly – James Spencer
p74 Badger – Jon Bowen
p80 Hickling Broad – Mike Page
p88 Balloo wetland – Ulster Wildlife Trust
p92 Camley Street – Anna Guzzo
p93 Camley Street Natural Park – London Wildlife Trust
p94 Land Art – Fen Oswin/Alamy
p96-7 River dipping – Emma Bradshaw/ emmabradshaw.blogspot.com
p102 Glow worm – John Tyler
p104-5 Flamborough Cliffs – David Nichols
p109 Dolphin – Janet Baxter
p111 Pooh sticks – Emma Bradshaw/ emmabradshaw.blogspot.com
p120 Beach clean – Bryan Whiting
p127 Pond-dipping – Derbyshire Wildlife Trust

p128 Basking shark – Andrew Pearson
p133 The Ercall/ Bluebell carpet – Shropshire Wildlife Trust
p134 Blackberrying – Emma Bradshaw/ emma bradshaw.blogspot.com
p138 Child at Penwortham Environment Education Centre – The Wildlife Trust for Lancashire, Manchester and North Merseyside
p142-3 Snorkel trail at Kimmeridge – Steve Trewhella
p154 Gors Maen Llwyd – Gavin Davies
p156-7 Knot at Gibraltar Point – Robin Cosgrove
p161 Grass snake – Ray Armstrong
p161 Adder – David Longshaw
p165 St George's Island – David Chapman/ davidchapman.org.uk
p179 Redpoll – Karen Summers
p179 Green-winged orchid – Paul Lane
p179 Knapp orchard – Paul Lane
p183 Common lizard – Neil Aldridge/ neilaldridge.wordpress.com
p184-5 Woods Mill – David Ball
p187 Lackford Lakes – Steve Aylward
p190 Scarlet tiger moth – Martin de Retuerto
p194 Pwll y Wrach waterfall – Brecknock Wildlife Trust
p196 Four spotted chaser – Helen Lacy
p199 Attenborough visitor centre – Nottinghamshire Wildlife Trust
p202 South Walney nature reserve – Cumbria Wildlife Trust
p206 Hanningfield Reservoir – Essex Wildlife Trust
p208 European beaver at Knapdale – Laurie Campbell/lauriecampbellphotography.com
p215 Blacka Moor – Roger Butterfield
p219 Hares Boxing – Gary K Smith / Alamy
p224-5 Peatland, Lancashire – Matthew Roberts